Basic
Model
Railroad
Benchwork

The Complete Photo Guide

Jeff Wilson

KALMBACH
BOOKS

Contents

Printed in the United States of America

12 11 10 09 08   3 4 5 6 7

Visit our website at http://kalmbachbooks.com
Secure online ordering available
ISBN13: 978-0-89024-615-3

Publisher's Cataloging-in-Publication

Wilson, Jeff.
    Basic model railroad benchwork / Jeff Wilson. — 1st ed.
    p. cm.
    Includes index.
    ISBN 0-89024-615-7

    1. Railroads—Models—Design and construction.
 I. Title.

TF197.W498 2002   625.1'9
                QBI02-200500

Art director: Kristi Ludwig
Cover design: Lisa Schroeder
Book design: Kory Beavers

Power tools you'll use throughout this book are indicated by the following symbols:

 Drill   **Miter saw**   **Jigsaw**   **Circular saw**

Introduction

BENCHWORK scares many people, but this need not be the case. Benchwork is among the most forgiving of all areas of building a model railroad. It's important to give your layout a sound foundation, but for the most part appearance is secondary, since virtually all of your benchwork will eventually be covered by track, scenery, and details.

The wide array of tools available today, including affordable power drills and saws, make it relatively easy to assemble benchwork for even large layouts in a matter of days.

You can get solid results even if you've never done a bit of woodworking before, provided you take your time and follow sound design and construction ideas and methods.

This book shows step-by-step photos with directions for building many styles of benchwork and approaching many situations you'll come across. However, it's best is to use this as an idea book—depending upon the space you're working with, different methods may be better choices than others.

You should have already established your track plan before designing and building your benchwork. There have been thousands of track plans published in magazines and books. Peruse them and look for a plan that you'd like to build. You can also design your own, either based on a published plan or completely new to suit own needs. As you do this I highly recommend getting a copy of John Armstrong's *Track Planning for Realistic Operation* (Kalmbach Publishing). It's an excellent guide to track and layout planning.

Whether you're using a published plan, modifying a plan, or drawing your own, here are a few points to consider:

• Keep all trackwork within arm's reach. This varies depending upon your size and reach and the height of the layout (the taller the layout, the shorter the convenient reach becomes). Even scenic elements located more than 30″ from the layout's edge will eventually need to be dusted, adjusted, or repaired, and if it's not convenient it won't get done. Any table wider than 36″ should have access from both sides.

• Avoid operating areas that are trapped within layouts. The reason that the shelf-style walkaround layout has become the norm for large layouts is that they're much easier to work on and operate. This is a consideration not only for operating, but for construction: How many times do you really want to get on the floor and crawl to a spot to build or run a layout?

• Avoid duckunders and lift-out sections as much as possible. They are often an attractive feature when drawing a track plan and sometimes they are unavoidable, but they can hinder operations.

• Avoid hidden staging areas if possible. If you must have hidden track, keep the track simple with as few turnouts as possible, and make sure you provide access to it to clean and repair track and fix derailments

• Be creative. This book can only suggest methods for accomplishing your goals. Use your imagination for tackling unique situations that confront you.

Many modelers ask what the best benchwork method is, but the answer is that there simply is no one best way to build benchwork. You can choose open-grid or L-girder, free-standing or attached to the walls, or a combination of styles—all can work well and will depend upon your final track plan.

Use the methods you feel will work best in your space and situation and the ones you're most comfortable doing. Now, let's get ready to go to the lumber yard, so we can get started!

Tools and materials

What you need to know before you get started

Starting work on a new layout is exciting. You have your track plan ready and you have a vision for what the scenery and completed layout will look like, but you have an important job to do first: provide a firm foundation for your model railroad.

Before starting construction, make sure you have a plan for the benchwork. The following chapters will help you design benchwork that will fit your space.

Make sure you have the necessary tools to do the job. Knowing how to use them can make a big difference in the quality of your work, and it can also save you a great deal of time.

It's a good idea to understand the materials you'll be working with. All 2 x 4s aren't created alike: There are many types of lumber and plywood, along with fasteners and other materials out there. Some work better than others in different situations, and knowing what does which job best can save you time, money, and frustration.

Let's get started with a look at tools.

ONCE CONSIDERED luxury items, power woodworking tools are now quite affordable. Power tools dramatically decrease the time required for a project and increase the quality of the finished product.

You don't need to go out and buy a $500 table saw to build quality benchwork, but a few smaller power tools will certainly be a great help.

Power drill/driver

A tool that I consider a necessity is a cordless drill and driver (fig. 1). It's among the most versatile and useful tools you can have around the house, and you'll use it for many tasks other than building benchwork.

Today's cordless drills have all the torque you'll need for both drilling holes and driving screws. Choose one with a ⅜" keyless chuck. It should also have at least

two speed settings (standard on most newer models).

Quality cordless drills are made by DeWalt, Ryobi, Black and Decker, and others. Most of the price differential is based on battery pack voltage. In general, the higher the voltage, the more torque it has and the longer the battery will last. Most drills come with two battery packs, so you can have one charging while you're using the other.

For most of us the 9-volt to 12-volt drills provide more than enough power. Drills up to 24 volts are favored by pros, who subject their tools to constant daily use. The tradeoff is that these battery packs are heavier, more awkward, and more expensive.

Avoid one-dimensional power screwdrivers. These tools often lack power and their design makes them awkward to use. You'll get much more bang for

your buck by buying a combination drill and driver.

You'll need several drill bits in various sizes. The sidebar on page 13 explains the different types of bits available and their uses.

Power saws

Number two on the power tool list is a saw. Table saws are extremely versatile, but they also take up a lot of space. Don't buy one just to build benchwork, but if you already have one you'll find it very handy, especially for ripping large sheet material

A better choice for many of us is a power miter saw. These make quick, precise cuts in strip material. The simplest ones (sometimes called "chop saws") do just that— pulling the blade down to the table cuts the material. The table rotates to make miter cuts at different angles.

Compound miter saws are a step

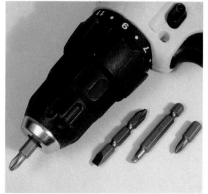

1 A combination cordless drill and driver, such as this DeWalt 9.6-volt model, is the handiest power tool you can own. Several types of driving bits are made, including reversible Phillips/standard, square drive, and single-head bits.

2 The table on a compound miter saw rotates to allow cuts at angles to just beyond 45 degrees.

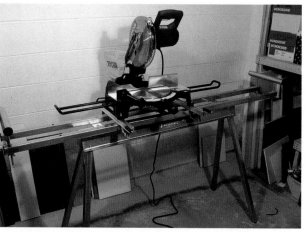

3 Saw tables, such as the TableMate, are handy for supporting lumber while it's being cut.

up, allowing you to adjust both the blade angle and the table. Figure 2 shows one from Ryobi, and fig. 3 shows a steel saw stand that does a good job of supporting the material being cut.

Check capacity when buying a miter saw. Smaller miter saws use 8″ blades; others have 10″ blades and can cut material up to 6″ wide and 4″ deep. And, if you really want to get fancy, sliding compound miter saws have blades that slide out on an arm, allowing them to cut material up to 10″ wide.

A jig saw or saber saw (fig. 4) is the handiest tool for cutting curves, such as when cutting roadbed or fascia contours. Blades

are measured in teeth per inch: the more teeth per inch the smoother the cut but the slower the cutting. Use 5 tpi for rough work; at least 10 tpi is good for smooth cuts.

If you don't have a table saw, use a circular saw for cutting large sheet material. See fig. 5. Most circular saws come with combination blades, making them useful for both ripping (cutting wood along the grain) and crosscutting (cutting across the grain).

Hand tools

With the many power tools on the market today it's easy to forget that hand tools are still very important in working with wood and other materials.

Handsaws. Figure 6 shows several types of handsaws. A good-quality crosscut handsaw will prove useful. Crosscut saws can be used for cutting dimensional lumber as well as plywood, and as the name implies, they are designed for cutting across the grain of the wood.

Like other saws, handsaws are measured in teeth per inch. Saws with many teeth per inch will cut slower but produce a cleaner cut; saws with fewer teeth per inch will cut quicker and more easily, but the cut edges will be rougher. I've found the Stanley 7 tpi saw in fig. 6 to be a good general-purpose saw, but I have a 10 tpi saw on hand for smoother cuts.

4 Handheld power jigsaws are used to cut curves in plywood, hardboard, and other material.

5 Circular saws can cut large sheet material and can also be used to trim dimensional lumber.

6 Common handsaws include (counterclockwise from front) 1, crosscut; 2, hacksaw; 3, drywall saw; and 4, coping saw.

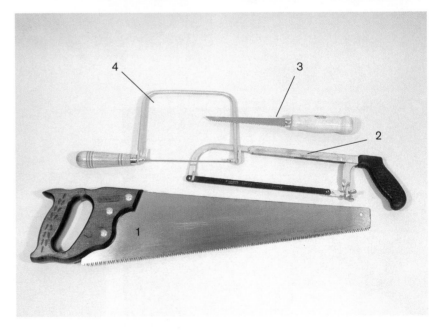

For making fine curved cuts by hand, use a coping saw. Figure 7 shows the proper technique for cutting with a coping saw. Note that coping saws are designed to cut with the saw pulling down—not being pushed like a crosscut saw.

Keyhole and drywall saws are designed for cutting holes in closed areas; they can be started by drilling a hole large enough for the saw blade to pass through. With these saws it's important not to get too exuberant—if the saw pops up through the hole the result is often a bent blade and—if you don't have your other hand clear—a nasty cut.

Hacksaws are designed for cut-ting metal. They have thin, replace-able blades with fine teeth.

If you don't have a power miter saw, you can use a hand miter saw for precision cuts. Figure 8 shows an inexpensive miter saw with a plastic miter box. The saw has fine teeth and a narrow profile, de-signed for use with the miter box. This box has grooves cut at 90 and 45 degrees. More expensive models have saws in a bracket above the cutting surface, and the bracket can be adjusted to any angle.

Saws (hand and power) can get hot during use, and a hot, dry blade tends to bind. Periodically oiling blades, as in fig. 9, will keep them working smoothly and will keep blades from rusting. Be sure to unplug power saws before oiling their blades.

Screwdrivers. The two most common types of screwdrivers are standard (slotted) and Phillips (cross pattern). However, screw-drivers come in a variety of sizes, with long and short shafts and blades in small, medium, and large sizes, as fig. 10 shows.

It pays to have at least two sizes of each on hand. Whether using a screwdriver or a power driver it's important to use the proper size bit, as fig. 11 shows. Using too large or too small a screwdriver can damage both the screwdriver and screw, as in fig. 12.

Squares. When building bench-work—or anything else in wood,

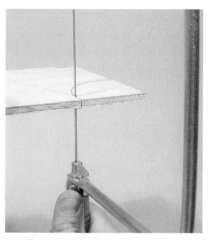

7 Coping saws are designed to cut while the user is pulling down, as when cutting a curved corner in this piece of plywood.

8 Small miter boxes typically have grooves cut at 90 and 45 degrees.

9 Oiling saw blades helps prevent binding while you cut and will keep them from rusting.

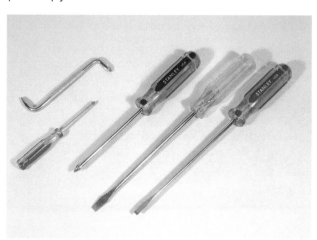

10 The curved-handle screwdriver at left is handy for getting into tight spaces.

11 Regardless of the type of head (slotted, Phillips, square, or other), the screwdriver blade should fit solidly in the notch of the screw.

12 Screwdrivers that are too big can slip and damage the screw or work surface. Using a screwdriver that is too small can damage the screwdriver.

for that matter—it's important to keep pieces square with each other. Figure 13 shows four types of squares. Combination and try squares are handy for marking 45- and 90-degree angles in dimensional lumber.

Framing (also called carpenter's) squares are handy for marking larger material and checking the square of pieces at a joint.

If you're marking or cutting a lot of plywood, foam, or other sheet material, you'll find a drywall square invaluable. As the name implies, it is designed for marking and cutting drywall, but it works well for any large sheet material. It has a four-foot arm and an 22″ T to reach all the way across a 4-foot-wide sheet of plywood.

Clamps. Clamps are used for holding pieces in place while you measure, level, and fasten them, and in building benchwork you'll find you'll need several. See fig. 14.

Traditional C-clamps are a popular choice, and are available in many sizes; 4″ jaws are the handiest for benchwork. Tightening the threaded rod grips the material in the clamp, resulting in a very strong joint. However, they can take a while to adjust and they can mar the surface being clamped, so use a thin piece of scrap wood between the clamp and the work.

Quick Grip clamps use a squeeze trigger to apply pressure, and a quick-action release lever allows sliding them in and out of position quickly. They have rubber-padded grips and won't hold as tightly as a C-clamp, but work for most benchwork applications. Like C-clamps, they are made in many sizes, with the 6″ capacity the most useful.

Miscellaneous tools. Figure 15 shows several other tools that you'll find handy. You'll need a claw hammer for driving (and removing) nails.

A good tape measure is indispensable. I have a 25-footer, which is very handy for checking room and overall layout dimensions, and a 16-footer, which is smaller and lighter, making it good for general use.

Files in a variety of lengths and shapes are handy for cleaning up edges on wood, as well as for carving contours.

A Stanley Surform plane is great for cleaning up rough edges on wood, rounding corners, and leveling joints.

You'll find a good utility knife much handier than a hobby knife for cutting and carving cardstock, thin wood, and other materials. Keep a supply of replacement blades, and if the blade chips or becomes dull, replace it.

Figure 15 also shows a palm-size rubber sanding block. I keep two handy, with coarse sandpaper on one and fine on the other.

13 Types of squares include try, combination, framing, and drywall squares.

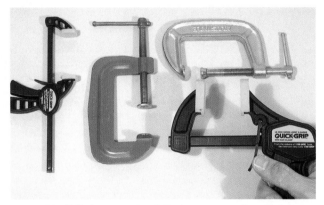

14 You'll find conventional C-clamps as well as Quick-Grip clamps handy for building benchwork.

15 Other handy tools include a hammer, tape measure, files, utility knives, Stanley Surform plane, and sanding block.

Drill Bits

Standard twist bits are good for general use in wood and metal. Steel bits are economical and will work well for wood; carbide bits are more expensive, but will last longer and are suitable for drilling metal.

Spade bits are flat with a point in the middle. They essentially drill their own pilot holes, then finish the hole. They make it possible to drill holes larger than the shaft capacity of your drill.

Forstner bits are another type of bit commonly used for drilling large holes. They have two advantages: They drill a very clean, round hole, and they are the bit to use if you need a hole with a flat bottom.

Use countersinking bits (fig. 28) when drilling pilot holes for flathead wood screws to set the head of the screw flush with the surface. These bits are available in numbers (4, 5, 6, 8, 10) to match wood screws, which use numbers to indicate the thickness of the shafts (the smaller the number, the narrower the shaft).

Since screws come in a variety of lengths, most countersinking bits have a small set screw on the side of the bit to permit adjusting for a deep or shallow hole.

Reversible bit/screwdrivers are very handy. They have a quick-change reversible head that has a countersinking bit on one end and a screwdriver blade on the other, making quick work of drilling pilot holes and driving screws. Many styles are available.

For starters I recommend buying a set of twist drills from 1/16" to 3/8", along with 1/2" and 3/4" spade bits and nos. 8 and 6 countersinking bits. You can buy an inexpensive set at first, then replace them with higher-quality carbide bits as the originals get dull.

Types of drill bits include spade, Forstner, twist, and twist with spade point.

Forstner bits are the best choice when you need a perfectly round hole or one with a flat bottom.

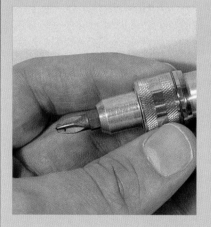

Quick-change reversible bits are very handy. This DeWalt bit has a collar that snaps in and out to release the head, which can be flopped end for end. The driver and drill bit are both replaceable, allowing you to change sizes and styles of bits as needed.

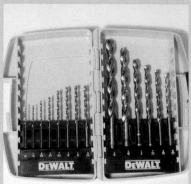

Bits are available in sets of commonly used sizes. It's handy to have a set that includes a case.

THE NUMBER OF construction materials and products available is staggering: lumber, plywood, OSB (oriented strand board), hardboard, and foam, to name just a few. In

16 Lumber dimensions

Nominal	Actual
1 x 2	¾" x 1½"
1 x 4	¾" x 3½"
1 x 6	¾" x 5½"
2 x 2	1½" x 1½"
2 x 4	1½" x 3½"
2 x 6	1½" x 5½"

addition to the materials themselves, an impressive array of glues is available, as well as screws, nails, and other hardware.

With such a variety it's important to understand what the different materials are designed for and what their strengths and weaknesses are.

A key point to remember is that most of what we do in assembling benchwork will be covered up by scenery. What's most important is that benchwork be sturdy, durable, and square, and there's no need to pay extra for cosmetic features that will later be hidden.

Most of our work is done with wood and wood-based products, so

we'll start by looking at lumber and other wood materials.

Dimensional lumber

Let's start with dimensional lumber. The first thing you'll find is that a finished 2 x 4 is not 2″ x 4″ (which is why lumber descriptions are never written with inch marks). A 2 x 4 is actually 1½″ x 3½″. Other true dimensions for dimensional lumber are in chart 16.

For benchwork we'll be using kiln-dried, untreated lumber. Lumber comes in several grades, based on the number and size of knots and the slope of the grain. Select (or select structural) is nearly

17 From top to bottom: Select, no. 2 and better, and no. 3 1 x 4s.

18 Avoid boards like this 1 x 2, which has a knot that severely compromises its strength.

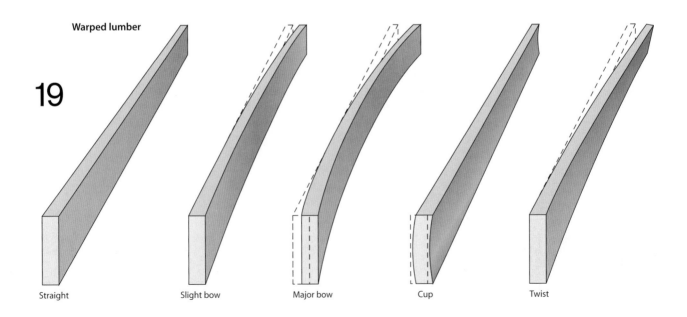

19

Warped lumber

Straight   Slight bow   Major bow   Cup   Twist

free of knots and has a broad grain slope; after that comes nos. 1, 2, and 3. Number 1 has the fewest and smallest knots and broadest grain; no. 3, more and larger knots and more grain curvature. Figure 17 shows a sample of each.

Select lumber can cost four or five times as much as no. 3, so use it only when appearance really matters. Numbers 1 and 2 are often grouped together (usually as "no. 2 and better"), and they're usually the best choice for benchwork. The knots are generally small, and it's usually not too difficult to find straight no. 2 and 3 boards.

Be picky about choosing wood.

The two most critical factors are that it be straight and that it not have any large knots or other defects which compromise its strength, like the board in fig. 18.

Figure 19 illustrates a straight board compared to those that are bowed, cupped, or twisted. Lumber that's bowed or cupped slightly can still be usable; however, if a board has a twist, discard it. A twisted board will throw off the squareness of an entire project.

Information on grades and type of wood are found either stamped on the wood itself or on a sticker or label. Information includes the size, grade, that it's S4S ("sanded

four sides"), and a moisture grade: S-Dry, meaning that the board has less than 19 percent water weight, or S-Grn (green), meaning that water content is higher than 19 percent. Be sure to buy the S-Dry variety to minimize shrinking.

When buying lumber, make sure that boards haven't spent time in a damp area of the lumber yard.

Dimensional lumber is prone to expansion and contraction along its length, caused mainly by variations in humidity. When you get lumber home, store it in your layout area for at least a few days to allow it to adjust to the temperature and humidity of its new environment.

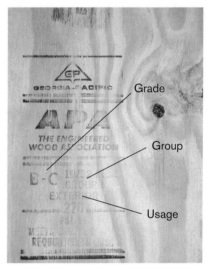

20 Plywood is made of three or more plies of wood glued and bonded under pressure. Shown here are standard ¼", ½", and ¾" pine or fir plywood.

21 Information stamped on plywood includes manufacturer, grade (B-C), size, species group (Group 1 is strongest), and whether it is rated for interior or exterior use.

22 Particle board (top) and OSB (bottom) are both made of sawdust and woodchips. Particle board is dense and smooth; OSB has a rougher texture.

23 Hardboard such as this ⅛" sheet has a smooth, hard surface on one or both sides.

PLYWOOD IS the most-used material for subroadbed and tabletop surfaces for good reasons: It's dimensionally stable, fairly easy to work with, and can easily be fastened by glue, screws, and nails. Plywood is also handy for shelves, fascia, control stands, and many other areas requiring flat sheet material.

Plywood is made up of several layers, or plies, of wood veneer glued on top of each other. See fig. 20. The grain in each succeeding layer is at a right angle to the one below it (except for four-layer plywood). This gives plywood excellent strength and makes it resistant to shrinkage caused by changes in temperature or humidity. Thicknesses range from ¼″ to ¾″ in ⅛″ increments.

Like dimensional lumber, plywood comes in several grades, with the information stamped on the board (fig. 21). You'll see a rating of A through D to describe the finish, with A the best and D the roughest. For example, A-C means that the top is finished and sanded, with knots filled, but the back is unfinished. Either A-C or B-C will work well for most benchwork uses.

One often-overlooked piece of information found on the stamp is the wood species group number. Use Group 1 plywood if possible, as it is the strongest and stiffest. Group 2 is the next best.

Particle board (fig. 22) is a heavy, dense board made from sawdust and woodchips and glued (bonded) together. Because it is dif-

24 Homasote is a fiberboard that's ideal for use as roadbed.

25 Extruded-foam insulation board comes in various thicknesses, including these 1½″ pink and 2″ blue boards.

ficult to easily drive staples, track nails, and other small fasteners into it, particle board is too hard for many benchwork uses. It is also much more prone to sagging than plywood, making it a poor choice for subroadbed and shelving.

Waferboard and strandboard (OSB), shown in fig. 22, are similar to particle board but use larger pieces of wood. These materials are designed for sheathing, and their hard, rough surfaces limit their use in benchwork.

Tempered hardboard (Masonite is one brand) is made from wood fibers and resins bonded under high pressure. The result is a very smooth, hard surface on one or both sides, as fig. 23 shows. Hardboard is an excellent choice for backdrops, fascia, and control panel facing. It comes in ⅛" and ¼" thicknesses.

Homasote (fig. 24) is a light-density fiberboard used as construction insulation. It is soft enough to push nails and track

spikes into, making it an excellent roadbed material. It also requires support to keep from sagging.

Foam board and drywall

Extruded polystyrene insulation—often called simply "foam board"—has become a popular material in scenery and sometimes in benchwork. It is lightweight, fairly strong, and easy to cut and work with hand tools. See fig. 25.

The material is usually blue or

26 The sides of drywall are beveled slightly to make it easier to join them with tape and joint compound.

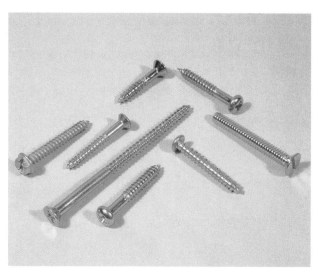

27 Screws come in many shapes and sizes, including wood screws with flat and round heads in Phillips or slotted styles. Some have combination slotted/hex heads. Bolts (far right) look similar, but aren't designed for use without a nut on the end.

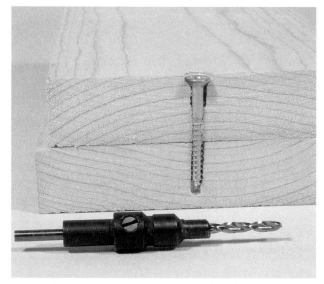

28 Drill pilot holes with a countersinking bit to get flat-head screws at or below surface level.

pink (sometimes gray) depending upon the manufacturer. It is typically available in 1″, 1½″, and 2″ thicknesses in 8-foot-long sheets in 16″, 18″, 24″, and 48″ widths. It can be difficult to find in warm Southern areas, but most large lumber yards and home centers stock it or can order it.

Foam is easy to cut with a knife (steak knives work well) or a saber saw with a knife blade. It can be shaped with Stanley Surform tools.

The best glues to use on foam are Liquid Nails for Projects, Woodland Scenics Foam Tack Glue, or water-based contact cement. Solvent adhesives (including plastic cement and cyanoacrylate

adhesive, or CA) will melt foam.

Drywall or plasterboard (Sheetrock is one brand) is a hard, dense board made of plaster sandwiched between paper sheets. See fig. 26. It is made from ¼″ to ⅜″ thick and can be used for backdrops and other vertical surfaces.

Fasteners

Nails aren't quite obsolete, but with the coming of the cordless drill/driver, screws have become the easiest way to secure joints. Screws hold more securely than nails, and it's easier to keep things in alignment with screws than when banging nails with a hammer.

Figure 27 shows a variety of

wood screws. Use flathead screws if you want the screwhead flush with the surface; round-head screws can be used in other places.

Screws are numbered based on diameter—the larger the number, the bigger the screw. Number 8 screws are adequate for most benchwork uses; no. 6 screws work in areas where not as much strength is required.

Drill pilot holes for wood screws, and countersink the hole when using flathead screws. See fig. 28. The pilot hole should be slightly smaller in diameter than the barrel of the screw.

Drywall screws (fig. 29) are designed to pull drywall tight

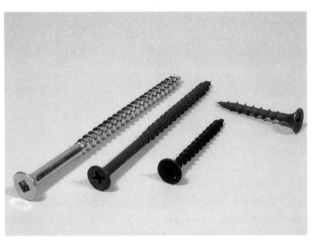

29 From left: a 3″ stainless steel deck screw with square drive head and coarse-thread drywall screws from 2½″ to 1¼″.

30 Hex and carriage bolts are available in a variety of lengths and shaft diameters. These ¼″ bolts are handy for benchwork.

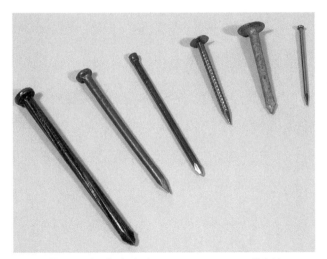

31 Types of nails include masonry, common, finishing, drywall, galvanized roofing, and wire.

32 Four of the most commonly used adhesives are white, carpenter's (aliphatic resin), polyurethane, and construction adhesive.

against wood, but they're inexpensive and handy for general-purpose use. They can be used to join wood to wood or any type of sheet material to wood. They're available with thin and coarse threads: The coarse threads go in faster and are less prone to stripping.

Use bolts when you need a very strong joint (such as fastening a leg to a frame or two frames to each other). See fig. 30. They're also a good choice when you need to make a piece easily removable.

Figure 31 shows several types of nails. Common nails have large heads and are designed for use where appearance isn't a factor. Finishing nails have small heads and are designed to be driven flush to the wood surface.

Adhesives

Figure 32 shows four of the most-used adhesives in building benchwork. For gluing wood to wood it's tough to beat yellow carpenter's glue. It's water-based and impervious to water once dry, sets quickly, and provides a very strong bond.

White glue has many of the same qualities, but doesn't contain the fillers of carpenter's glue and isn't as strong. It's still good for lesser duties such as gluing roadbed to subroadbed.

For joining dissimilar materials use a construction adhesive such as Liquid Nails. There are many types, including Liquid Nails for Projects, which is safe to use on plastics and foam board, and Heavy Duty Liquid

Nails, handy for bonding wood to concrete walls or floors.

Polyurethane glue expands as it dries, filling gaps and providing a strong bond joining wood to nonporous materials such as metal and coated particle board (such as Melamine).

Dehumidifiers

Most problems with expansion and contraction on a layout are caused by humidity changes. Problems can include cracked scenery, gaps or kinks in rails, buckled subroadbed, and liftout sections or swinging gates that no longer fit properly.

These problems are exacerbated in basements, where humidity can range from under 20 percent in the winter to more than 70 percent in the summer. If you have a layout in a basement, even one that seems dry, it's wise to run a dehumidifier during the humid summer months. Keep a humidity gauge near your layout, and if the gauge goes above 50 percent, turn up the dial on the humidifier.

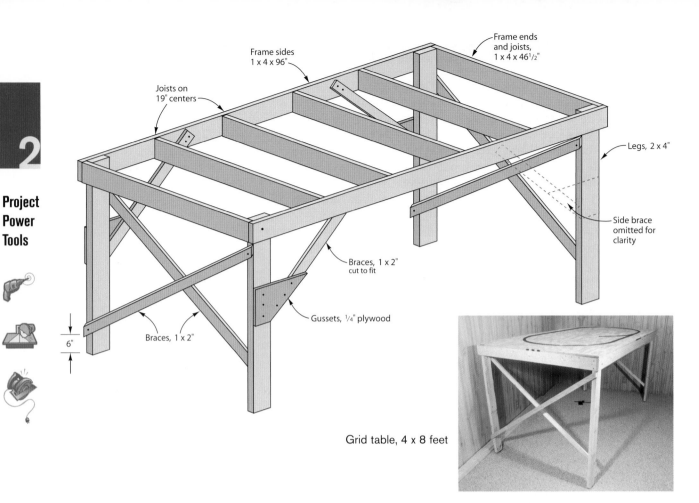

Frame sides
1 x 4 x 96"

Frame ends
and joists,
1 x 4 x 46½"

Joists on
19" centers

Legs, 2 x 4

Side brace
omitted for
clarity

Braces, 1 x 2"
cut to fit

Gussets, ¼" plywood

6"

Braces, 1 x 2"

Grid table, 4 x 8 feet

Simple grid table

A solid base for a small layout

A basic free-standing table was the first layout for many—if not most—model railroaders. It seems logical: Plywood comes in 4 x 8-foot sheets, so building a table underneath it is an easy way to get a layout up and running.

Table layouts do have many advantages: They're easy to build. Access is generally open all around them. And if your goal is to build a portable layout, a table style is the easiest to set up and take down.

However, table layouts have many drawbacks as well. They take a huge amount of space—something not apparent when you're looking at a 4 x 8 sheet of plywood. To make that 4 x 8 layout fit in a room and be usable, you'll need at least 2 (and preferably) 3 feet of space around it on all sides,

meaning that 4 x 8 layout needs about 10 x 14 feet of space.

Track plans are rather limited, since curves must be necessarily tight to keep the track on the table. It's difficult to add dramatic scenic elements, such as a turntable and roundhouse or mountain, because large individual elements tend to dominate the layout and not allow room for much else.

If you decide to go with a table, there are many designs to choose from. Grid tables (sometimes also called "butt-joint" tables) are ideal if you're looking for a simple square or rectangular layout. If you want a layout with curved sides, or if you need a table longer than 12 to 14 feet, check out the L-girder design shown in the next chapter.

A 1 X 4 FRAME is more than solid enough to support scenery and trains in any scale. The diagram on page 20 shows a drawing of the basic table assembly. Before beginning construction, measure your tabletop. Sheets of plywood sometimes vary slightly in dimensions.

Begin by cutting the framing pieces. With butt-joint assembly it's critical that the ends of the 1 x 4 joists, ends, and sides be square, so use a miter saw to make all of the cuts.

Assemble the framing to support the table, starting with the outer 1 x 4s. As fig. 1 shows, drill countersunk pilot holes at the ends of each side 1 x 4. Add glue to the end of an end piece as in fig. 2, then screw the side piece in place (fig. 3). I used 1¾" wood screws, but drywall screws will work as well. Repeat until you have the outer frame assembled.

Before adding the cross pieces (joists), check your track plan for any recessed areas. It's possible to

do modifications later, but it's easier to adjust the interior framing now, if possible. Also, try to avoid having turnouts directly above joists.

Mark the center of each joist along each side, as fig. 4 shows. When adding joists, make sure that each is vertical by clamping a try square in place as a guide, as fig. 5 shows. Glue and screw the ends of each.

Figure 6 shows the completed frame with joists in place.

1 Drill three countersunk holes at the ends of each side 1 x 4 to attach the end pieces.

2 Run a bead of carpenter's glue on the end of the end piece before screwing it in place.

3 Screw the side to the end using 1¾" no. 8 wood screws.

4 Mark the center of each joist at the top of each side.

5 Clamp a try square in place, then hold the joist against the square as you screw it into place.

6 The completed frame is ready for legs and bracing.

I USED 48″-TALL LEGS, but you may want to choose a different height. See the sidebar on page 23 for a discussion of layout height.

Since very few basement floors are level, it's good to provide a way of leveling the table once it's in place. An easy way to do this is to use T-nuts and adjustable mounting feet, as fig. 7 shows. The mounting feet are also easier on carpeted floors than raw wood. If your floor is concrete, you can sub-stitute inexpensive carriage bolts.

Drill a hole in the bottom center of each leg to match the threaded rod of the mounting foot. Smaller T-nuts have barbs that must be pounded in place with a hammer; larger ones like those in fig. 7 have screw mounting holes. Once the T-nuts are installed, screw the feet in place.

Use a C-clamp or Quick Grip to clamp each leg to hold it in place. (It's handy to have a helper for this.) See fig. 8. Use a framing square to make sure the leg is per-pendicular to the frame, then drive a couple of screws through the end into the leg to secure it, as fig. 9 shows.

Drill a ¼″ hole through the side 1 x 4 and the leg for a carriage bolt, as in fig. 10. Push the bolt into place from outside the frame, add a washer and a nut, and tighten it with a wrench or socket.

7 Start by marking the center of the end of the leg. Drill a hole to clear the bolt, then add the T-nut followed by the mounting feet (or carriage bolt).

8 Use C-clamps or Quick-Grips to hold the legs in place.

9 Drive two wood screws through the ends into each leg.

10 Add a ¼" bolt to secure each leg. Tighten the nut securely with a wrench.

Layout height

Before building a layout of any type—tabletop or around-the-walls—you need to determine the layout's height. Layout height has been a subject of debate in the model railroad press for years. The current trend is toward eye-level position of trains, giving the most realistic (ground-level) view. However, many modelers favor a slightly lower height (chest-level) that allows viewing more of a scene and makes it easier to work on the layout.

Many factors enter into the layout height debate, including your height, the type of layout you're building (Midwestern plains or Rocky Mountains), whether you plan to operate your layout standing or sitting, the height of your ceiling, and whether you have significant grades.

Large walkaround-style layouts are generally built taller than table layouts, because the operators are standing or walking while running trains. For a small room or free-standing layout where operators are sitting, a lower height might be better.

Although it's fun to watch trains at eye level, tall layouts can be awkward for operators if hand uncoupling tools or hand-thrown turnouts are used. Also, the taller the layout, the more difficult it is to reach in to work on scenery or fix any problems.

If your layout is built on a continuous grade, you may have to start at a fairly low level and continue to a tall height in order to keep the grade going.

Consider all of the factors and choose a height that will work best for you.

END BRACES MADE of 1 x 2s or furring strips will stabilize the table. Whenever you're designing or adding bracing, think in triangles. The lower the braces extend on the legs, the stronger the braces will be.

Clamp a 1 x 2 in place diagonally across one end and mark the brace to provide a guide for cutting, as fig. 11 shows. Cut the brace, clamp it in place, check the leg with a framing square, and screw the brace in place as in fig. 12 Add the remaining end braces.

Figure 13 shows the table with the braces in place. I was hoping that the 2 x 4 legs would make the table solid enough without side braces, but it still swayed just enough to be unacceptable.

To fix this I used fairly short braces on the sides, which made the table quite solid but were unobtrusive enough to provide good under-table access for wiring and storage.

Cut the 1 x 2 front braces to fit, as fig. 14 shows. The top of each brace is screwed to the inside of the frame, with a gusset plate of ¼" plywood to secure the braces to the legs.

You could get away with 2 x 2s for legs on a table like this one, but you'll need side braces that extend from the bottom of each leg to the midpoint of the sides.

11 Clamp a 1 x 2 in place for the end brace and mark it for cutting.

12 Use a single 1¾" no. 8 wood screw to secure each end of the end braces.

13 The end braces are in place and the table is nearly complete.

14 Cut the lower end of each side brace at an angle to match the legs. Screw a ¼" plywood gusset plate in place to secure the brace and leg.

IF YOU PLAN to elevate your track by using the cookie-cutter method or with risers and free-form sub-roadbed, you can stop now and turn to Chapters 4 and 5. If you just want a simple tabletop, read on.

The first temptation is to simply attach the plywood top by driving screws down through the top into the joists. However, this makes it difficult to make changes once the track and scenery are in place. Attaching the top with cleats will make later alterations—including

cutting and elevating the sub-roadbed and other features— much easier.

Add 1 x 1 or 1 x 2 cleats as fig. 15 shows. Drill countersunk pilot holes vertically through the center of each before installing it.

Locate the cleats around the perimeter of the layout every 16" or so, and use one or two on each intermediate joist. Clamp each cleat in place so the top is flush with the top of the joist. Use 1¾" (with 1 x 2s) or 1¼" wood or

drywall screws to secure them.

Once the plywood top is in place, drive 1" coarse-thread drywall screws (1¼" if using ⅝" plywood) up through the cleats to anchor the table top (fig. 16).

If you do choose to simply add screws from above, be sure to countersink the holes so that screw heads don't interfere with track or other details, as in fig. 17.

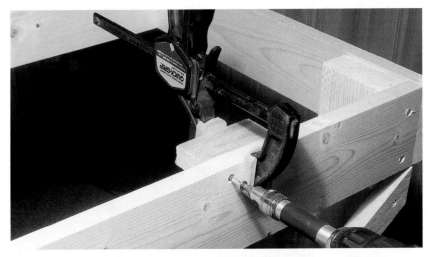

15 Clamp cleats made from 1 x 2s or 1 x 1s in place, then use two screws to secure each.

16 Secure the plywood top by driving screws upward through each cleat.

17 If you use any screws on top of the table, be sure to countersink the holes so that the screw heads are recessed.

ALTHOUGH 4 X 8 FEET is the most common size for a table like this, you can adjust the size to suit your space. You can buy 1 x 4s in 10-, 12-, and 14-foot lengths; fig. 18 shows plans for tables of those lengths.

Note how all tables longer than 8 feet have the legs set in from the ends; if there's more than 18" of overhang on the ends, add braces from the legs to the ends.

I wouldn't recommend building a grid table longer than 12 feet. For long tables a better choice is the L-girder design shown in the next chapter, which allows building tables up to 20 feet long with just four legs.

Smaller tables can follow the same design as the table on page 20. For tables 3 x 6 feet and smaller you can substitute 1 x 3s for the frame.

Materials for 10-foot table

Lumber	Hardware
1 x 2, 8-foot, 8	¼" x 3" carriage bolts, nuts, washers, 4
1 x 4, 10-foot, 2	
1 x 4, 8-foot, 4	no. 8 x 1¾" screws, 56
½" plywood, 4 x 8 feet, 1	no. 8 x 1¼" screws, 16
½" plywood, 2 x 4 feet, 1	no. 8 x ¾" screws, 12
¼" plywood, scraps for gussets	T-nuts with threaded feet, 4, optional

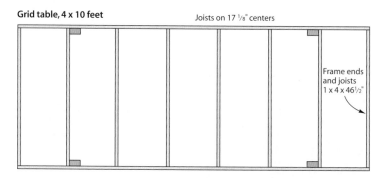

Grid table, 4 x 10 feet. Joists on 17 ⅛" centers. Frame ends and joists 1 x 4 x 46½"

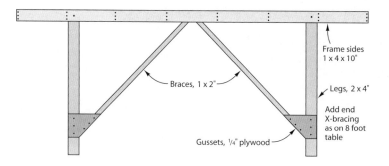

Frame sides 1 x 4 x 10". Braces, 1 x 2". Legs, 2 x 4". Gussets, ¼" plywood. Add end X-bracing as on 8 foot table

Materials for 12-foot table

Lumber	Hardware
1 x 2, 8-foot, 8	¼" x 3" carriage bolts, nuts, washers, 4
1 x 4, 12-foot, 2	
1 x 4, 8-foot, 5	no. 8 x 1¾" screws, 62
½" plywood, 4 x 8 feet, 1	no. 8 x 1¼" screws, 32
½" plywood, 4 x 4 feet, 1	no. 8 x ¾" screws, 24
¼" plywood, scraps for gussets	T-nuts with threaded feet, 4, optional

18

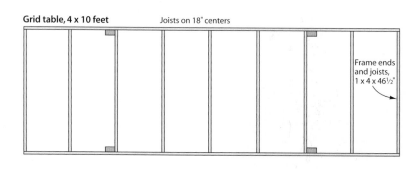

Grid table, 4 x 10 feet. Joists on 18" centers. Frame ends and joists, 1 x 4 x 46½"

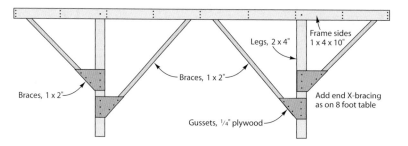

Legs, 2 x 4". Frame sides 1 x 4 x 10". Braces, 1 x 2". Braces, 1 x 2". Gussets, ¼" plywood. Add end X-bracing as on 8 foot table

Hollow-core door table

A simple portable layout table can be made from an inexpensive hollow-core door. Tables made in this manner are inexpensive, lightweight, portable, and amazingly strong.

Since common door widths go up to 36", this method is mainly for N scale, but can also work for a small switching or display layout in HO or larger scales.

When buying a door, look for the least expensive one, since you won't be seeing the finish. You might be able to save a few bucks by asking if there are any slightly damaged doors hiding in the storeroom.

The legs are the common folding variety (many styles are made) available at hardware and home centers. You can buy these new, or you might be able to salvage a pair from an old folding table.

The photos show the basic construction. The key to remember is that these doors consist of thin sheets of lauan plywood with a honeycomb paper interior, so other than the wood around the edges there's nothing solid.

Because of this, anchor the legs to 1 x 4s that have been screwed to the edge pieces on the door.

Once the table itself is complete, paint the surface to seal it and prevent any damage from water-based scenery. As the photo shows, you can also glue a piece of 1½" or 2" foam board to the table as a base for the layout.

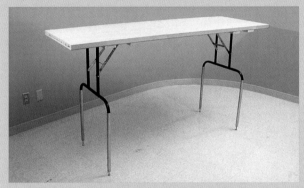

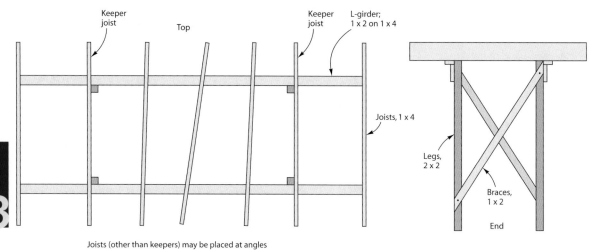

Keeper joist

Top

Keeper joist

L-girder; 1 x 2 on 1 x 4

Joists, 1 x 4

Legs, 2 x 2

Braces, 1 x 2

End

Joists (other than keepers) may be placed at angles

Braces, 1 x 2

Gussets, ¼" plywood

Side

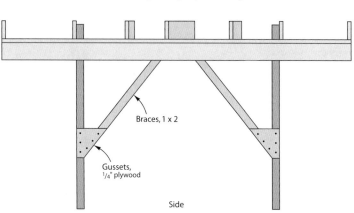

L-girder benchwork

A versatile base for larger layouts

Materials for 8-foot L-girder table

Lumber	Hardware
1 x 3, 8-foot 2 (for girders; 1 x 4 can also be used)	¼" x 3" carriage bolts, nuts, and washers, 4
1 x 4, 8-foot, 4 (for joists)	no. 8 x 1¾" screws, 30
1 x 2, 8-foot, 2	no. 8 x ¾" screws, 24
2 x 2, 8-foot, 2	T-nuts with threaded feet (optional), 4
½" plywood, 4 x 8 feet, 1	
¼" plywood, scraps for gussets	

Developed by former *Model Railroader* editor Linn Westcott in the 1950s, L-girder benchwork has become very popular for good reason. It's sturdy, easy and quick to assemble, and economical in use of wood; it can support long spans (up to 20 feet) with just four legs.

The heart of the design is the girder itself, made by fastening a 1 x 2 flange atop a piece of 1 x 2, 1 x 3, or 1 x 4. The flange gives the girders remarkable strength and also allows adding joists at any location by means of screws driven up from the bottom through the flange.

The L-girder design is an excellent choice for long table-style layouts as well as around-the-walls model railroads, and adapts well to wall-mounted benchwork, as Chapter 9 shows.

The drawing on this page shows the basics of L-girder construction in a simple 4 x 8-foot table.

The joists can be used to support a plain tabletop, a cookie-cutter top, or free-flowing subroadbed on risers. The L-girder design has great flexibility, as the joists can be easily be positioned at any convenient location and at any angle to allow for rivers, roads, towns, and other elements.

LET'S GO STEP-BY-STEP through building the 4 x 8 table in on page 28. When designing an L-girder layout, most critical dimensions are fifths: The leg assemblies should each be set in ⅕ of the total length, and the L-girders should be set in ⅕ the length of the joists (although some joists may overhang farther than this).

You can use 2 x 4s for legs, but with sufficient bracing, 2 x 2s are more than adequate. It's important to attach the leg bracing as close to the floor on the legs as possible.

Start with the leg assemblies. I didn't do it on this layout, but I highly recommend adding levelers to the bottom of each leg, as shown in Chapter 2. Doing so will make it much easier to level the table if the floor isn't quite level (and few floors are).

Measure and mark a spot ⅕ of the way in from each end of the joist (9½″ for a 4-foot-wide layout). Set the legs in relation to these marks so that the top of each leg is just shy of the top of the joist. See fig. 1.

Drill a pilot hole and add one screw to hold each leg in place. See fig. 2. Use a framing level to make sure that each leg is square with the joist (fig. 3), then add the second screw to secure each leg.

Add the first diagonal brace. Cut each end of the brace using a miter saw, then use a single screw at each end to secure it. Before adding the screw at the base of the each leg, check the leg once again with the square. See fig. 4.

Flip the assembly over and add the second diagonal brace on the

1 Begin by positioning a joist atop the legs.

2 Add one screw through the joist into the leg.

3 Check the leg with a framing square.

4 Add the first diagonal brace, then flip the assembly over and add the second brace.

other side of the legs. Figure 5 shows a finished leg assembly.

Time for the girder itself. When picking lumber for L-girder lay-outs, be sure to choose the straightest boards possible for the girders and flanges.

Begin making an L-girder by running a bead of carpenter's glue along the top of the vertical girder, then use several clamps to hold the flange in place, as fig. 6 shows. Use drywall or wood screws to attach the flange.

I used 1 x 4s with 1 x 2 caps for this table, but 1 x 3s would have been sufficient—I just didn't have any handy.

Once the girders are made, clamp them to the leg assemblies as fig. 7 shows. The basic table is now complete—all that's left is to add the bracing and remaining joists.

Make sure that the girders are level with each other. Drive a 2″ no. 8 wood screw through the girder into each leg, then use the framing square again to make sure the legs are square to the girders before adding a second screw. See fig. 8. You could also use a single ¼″ carriage bolt if you prefer.

Add the side diagonal braces. Use ¼″ plywood gusset plates as figs. 9 and 10 show to secure the bottoms

5 The first leg assembly is ready.

6 Spread glue along the top of the 1 x 4, then clamp the 1 x 2 flange in place. Use screws to hold the girder together.

7 Clamp the girders to the finished leg assemblies.

8 Make sure the leg assemblies are square to the girders before screwing them in place.

of the braces to the legs. Figure 11 shows how the tops of the braces meet at the middle of the table inside of the L-girders.

Figure 12 shows how to anchor the joists. Drill a pilot hole and drive a screw through the flange into the bottom of the joist. If you're building a simple tabletop, you can secure the joists now; if you're using a cookie-cutter or open style, then don't screw the joists in place yet. Instead, wait until you know where track and complex scenic details will be located.

For details on cookie-cutter table construction, see Chapter 4, and for free-form subroadbed on risers see Chapter 7. Chapter 10 shows how to add a fascia to an L-girder layout.

9 Clamp the gusset plate in place.

10 Use screws to secure the brace to the leg.

11 Use two screws to secure the top of each brace to the inside of the girder.

12 Drive a screw from under the L-girder flange to secure each joist at each end.

THE TABLE I HAVE just discussed is 4 x 8 feet, but you can adjust the height, length, and width to suit your own needs—the construction steps remain the same. Figure 13 shows the maximum length for various girders, with guides to leg placement and allowable span distance. As the chart shows, you can stretch the table to more than 20 feet with only four legs.

One of L-girder's strengths is that it can be used to design odd-shaped areas. Since there's no outside frame, joists can be different lengths, so if you want the layout wider or narrower at an area—to accommodate an aisle, for example—you can cut joists longer or shorter.

Figure 14 shows a couple of examples of how to do this. Chapter 10 explains how to add a fascia that will give the layout edge a smooth, flowing appearance.

Some joists can overhang their girder by more than ⅕ their total length, but if you have several that need to be longer it's wise to build an outrigger assembly, as fig. 15 shows. This is also handy for building short perpendicular extensions at the ends of tables.

Making the end of a table wide for a turnback curve is another possibility. Figure 16 shows one

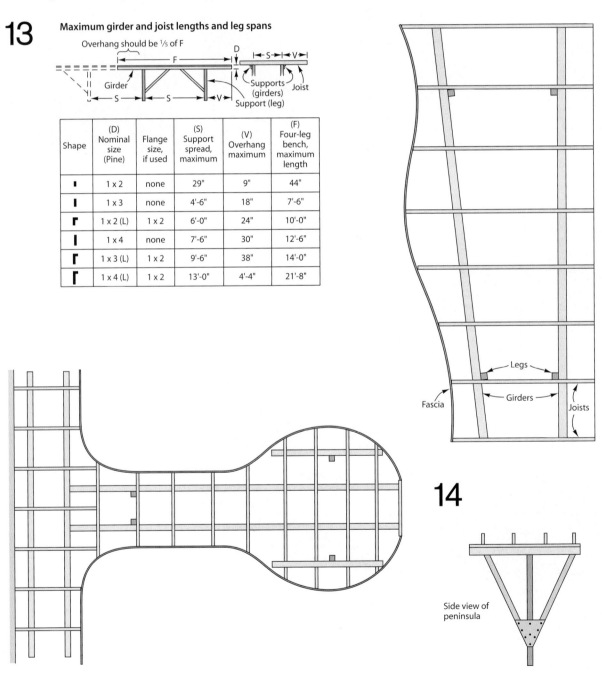

13 Maximum girder and joist lengths and leg spans

Overhang should be ⅕ of F

Girder · Supports (girders) · Joist · Support (leg)

Shape	(D) Nominal size (Pine)	Flange size, if used	(S) Support spread, maximum	(V) Overhang maximum	(F) Four-leg bench, maximum length
▮	1 x 2	none	29"	9"	44"
Ⅰ	1 x 3	none	4'-6"	18"	7'-6"
Γ	1 x 2 (L)	1 x 2	6'-0"	24"	10'-0"
Ⅰ	1 x 4	none	7'-6"	30"	12'-6"
Γ	1 x 3 (L)	1 x 2	9'-6"	38"	14'-0"
Γ	1 x 4 (L)	1 x 2	13'-0"	4'-4"	21'-8"

Legs · Girders · Joists · Fascia

14

Side view of peninsula

way of doing this. In both of these examples the joists can later be hidden by a fascia, as described in Chapter 10.

When you're building long tables or layout sections, it is necessary to splice the L-girders. You can buy 1 x 4s up to 14 feet long, but that might not be practical for you, and it might still not be long enough for your longest run.

Figure 17 shows how to splice a girder. If possible, stagger the joints on the flange and web. It's not necessary to add a splice plate on the flange, just the web. Use a 1 x 4 plate on the outside of the L; the length of the plate should be a least four times the depth of the web.

Doing this allows using a smaller splice plate of ¼" plywood on the inside of the L. This adds stability to the joint and still allows room for

driving screws through the flange into joists above the splice plates.

Building a larger layout with L-girder benchwork is just a matter of interconnecting tables like these. Chapter 8 includes more details on using wall-mounted brackets to support an L-girder assembly, including designs for corners as well as ideas for adding peninsulas with L-girders.

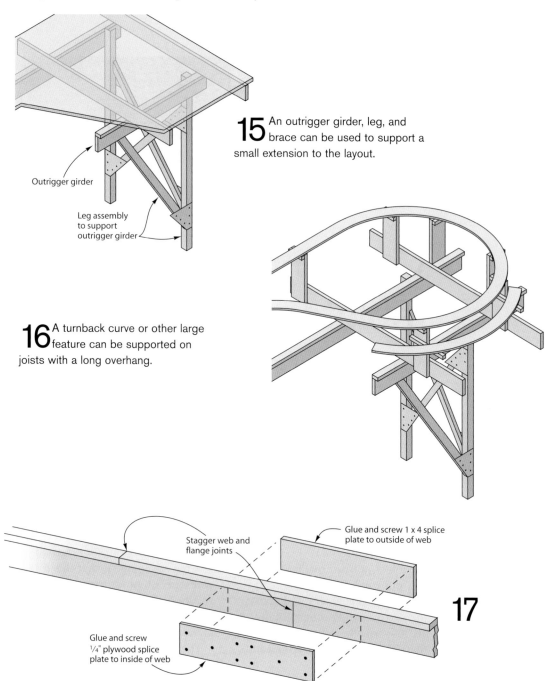

15 An outrigger girder, leg, and brace can be used to support a small extension to the layout.

Outrigger girder

Leg assembly to support outrigger girder

16 A turnback curve or other large feature can be supported on joists with a long overhang.

Stagger web and flange joints

Glue and screw 1 x 4 splice plate to outside of web

Glue and screw ¼" plywood splice plate to inside of web

17

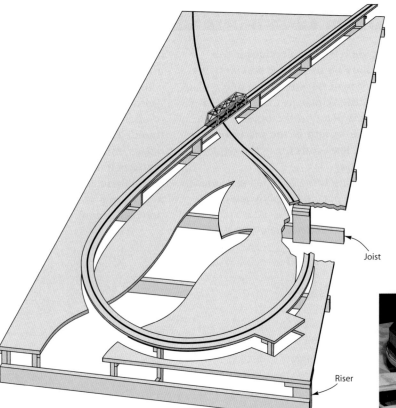

Joist

Riser

Cookie-cutter tabletop

An easy way to add depth to a layout

For many beginning modelers a table with a plain tabletop is the obvious first choice, but it can also be quite limiting. A flat table makes it handy to try different track arrangements and place buildings and other details, but scenery doesn't get interesting until you start to vary the elevations of the track and other elements.

Look at railroad roadbed in real life, and you'll find that railroad tracks are usually elevated above the surrounding scenery. Highways are also usually elevated. Then there are hills, ravines, rivers, and other details, as well.

To get this grade variation, the first impulse might be to add risers on top of the flat table. However,

it's difficult to get a smooth grade transition this way, and operation (and appearance) can suffer.

Among the best methods of getting separations in elevation is the cookie-cutter technique, illustrated above. After outlining the track and roadbed on the plywood, you cut away the area to elevate or recess the track, roads, or other details.

A big advantage is that this provides a continuous layer of sub-roadbed, allowing smooth grade transitions and grades as steep or gradual as you need.

The cookie-cutter method is very flexible. You can leave the table portion in place for towns and large industries, or remove it or recess it for low areas.

LET'S TAKE A step-by-step look at applying the cookie-cutter technique to a table layout. The first step is to draw your track plan on the plywood. We'll do this on the ½″ plywood top on the table built in Chapter 2.

Draw track centerlines, using a long ruler or straightedge for straight sections. To draw curves you can make a compass from a wood yardstick, as fig. 1 shows. Drill a hole at the 1″ mark large enough to place over a wire nail at the center of the curve. Drill additional holes at locations to match the radius of your track—for example, 19″ for 18″ radius curves (the

extra inch makes up for the lost inch at the end).

Tack a wire nail in place on the table at the center of the curve. Place the end hole of the yardstick on the nail, then use the pencil through the appropriate hole to draw the curve.

Whether you're following a published plan or designing your own, it's a good idea to lay the track in place to make sure it fits following the plan. See fig. 2. This isn't as vital if you're using flextrack for curves, but if you're using sectional track, it's important to make sure it matches what you've planned.

You should also do this in areas

of complex trackwork where multiple turnouts or crossings come together. Figure 3 shows how to use photocopies of turnouts on a sheet of paper to help lay out these areas.

Once the track is in place, use a pencil to sketch other details, such as roads, streets, sidewalks, and structures, as well as scenery details such as lakes and rivers. See fig. 4.

When you're sure of the locations of these details, use a felt-tip marker to highlight just those lines that need to be cut (fig. 5). For grade-separated crossings between roads and tracks keep the railroad

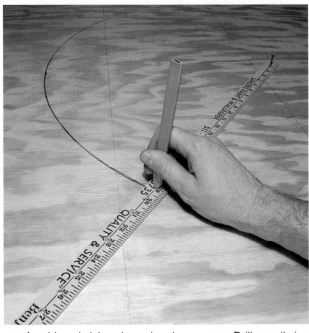

1 An old yardstick makes a handy compass. Drill pencil-size holes at every inch mark for which you need curves.

2 Test-fit the track in place. Map pins are handy for holding it in place.

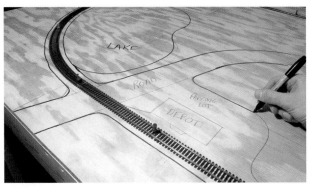

3 Photocopies of turnouts work well for testing. Note how much more room the photocopies take than the original track centerlines at left.

4 Pencil in details like roads, structures, lakes, and rivers.

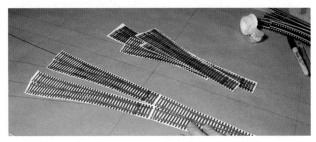

5 Use a felt-tip marker to outline the areas to be cut.

roadbed solid and cut the road; for grade-separated railroad-over-railroad crossings, keep the upper line intact and cut the lower line. They can be spliced later.

You can leave the plywood in place and use a saber saw to cut along the marked lines, as in fig. 6. Raise the plywood above the table frame with 2 x 2 scraps to keep the saw from cutting the frame.

The lake in fig. 7 should be recessed below the table surface.

The complexity of this depends upon the location of the frame members. As the photo shows, there was a single joist under the lake.

Start by marking the depth of the cut on the joist—I cut mine an inch below the top. Cut this with a saber saw. If you cut down more than half the depth of a joist, then reinforce it as the drawing in fig. 8 shows.

As you cut the subroadbed, you'll find areas where you need to add additional cross joists. Figure 9 shows where I added two to support the lake and the track sub-roadbed around the curve.

Cut notches in the joists below the lake to match the original joist. Screw the new joists in place. A general rule of thumb is to support the roadbed at least every 16" to 18". Figure 10 shows the lake cutout—now the lake bed—in place on the cut-out joists.

6 Use lumber scraps to elevate the plywood, then make the cuts with a saber saw.

7 Mark the joist under the lake area at the proper depth.

9 The joist has been cut and two additional cross joists have been added.

10 Screw the lake bed in place, being sure to countersink the screw heads.

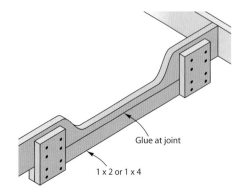

Glue at joint

1 x 2 or 1 x 4

8 Attach additional supports to a joist notched more than half its depth.

FIGURE 11 SHOWS how flexible the plywood is once the sub-roadbed and other details are cut to elevate the cookie-cut roadbed. To secure it at the desired height, you'll need to add blocks of wood called risers to the joists. Cut-off scraps of 1 x 2 and 1 x 4 lumber make ideal risers.

Start by clamping a riser under the roadbed at the highest elevation (fig. 12). Make sure that the roadbed is level and that the top of the riser is in full contact with the underside of the roadbed. You can then screw the riser in place.

Follow this by adding risers on the grade. When you have all the risers in the proper position and the grade is smooth, secure the roadbed to the risers. See fig. 13.

For cookie-cutter tops where it's not likely that the subroadbed location will change, you can simply drive a screw through the roadbed into the top of the riser, as fig. 14 shows. Make sure the pilot hole is countersunk so that the screwhead is completely below the sub-roadbed surface.

If you think you might make later changes, you can use risers with cleats, as described in Chapter 7.

11 Once cut, the plywood becomes quite easy to move.

12 Clamp a 1 x 2 riser in place at the highest elevation, but don't screw it into place.

13 Add the intermediate risers. When all are in place, screw the risers to the joists.

14 Screw the plywood to the risers. Make sure the screwheads are below surface level.

IF YOU'RE PLACING a cookie-cutter top on an L-girder table, it's a bit easier to add low-level details, such as rivers and roads, that run off of the layout edge. To do this, cut out the river at the width and shape you need. It can be secured to the girders themselves (fig. 15) or to lower-profile joists. See fig. 16.

Figure 17 shows the entire area on an L-girder table—the basic cookie-cutter technique is the same on each.

15 On an L-girder frame, low-level items such as riverbeds can be secured directly to the girders (as in the left photo) or on shallow joists (as at right).

16 Note how the joists don't have to be perpendicular to the girders.

17 The cookie-cutter technique works the same on an L-girder base as on a grid base. The extra framing on the edge of the table is for a fascia to be added later.

SCENERY BASED ON extruded-foam insulation board has been popular for some time, and it is being used more and more in benchwork applications such as subroadbed and tabletops.

Its advantages include its light weight and its ability to be cut and shaped without power tools, a big advantage if you live in an apartment or other area where use of power tools is discouraged.

You can also do a variation of the cookie-cutter method by using various thicknesses of sheet extruded foam on a table. The basic idea is shown in fig. 18. The top sheet of foam serves as the tabletop, and you can carve away foam to make ditches, ravines, and rivers.

You can use a simple frame table to support the foam. I recommend using a thin (¼") sheet of plywood between the frame and foam.

Doing this will increase the strength of the table and provide a solid base for the foam.

To elevate the track you can cookie-cut the top piece of foam as shown below, using scraps of foam as risers. You can cut foam with a conventional kitchen or steak knife (utility knives usually don't have long enough blades). Woodland Scenics and others also offer hot-wire tools for cutting and shaping

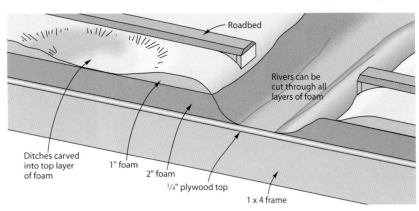

Roadbed

Rivers can be cut through all layers of foam

Ditches carved into top layer of foam

1" foam

2" foam

¼" plywood top

1 x 4 frame

18 You can cookie-cut foam just like plywood. One-inch foam works best this way. A steak or kitchen knife works well to cut foam. Once the foam is cut, it can be elevated or depressed.

foam, or you can use a saber saw with a knife (leather-cutting) blade.

Another variation on this theme uses commercial grades and risers offered by Woodland Scenics. Figure 19 shows a couple of these products. The line includes flexible foam pieces with 2- and 4-percent grades, along with flexible sub-roadbed pieces ("risers") that keep track elevated above the surface.

These pieces are designed to be glued atop a foam tabletop, covered by plaster gauze, and sanded smooth; they are then ready for roadbed. Figures 20 and 21 show them being used on a *Model Railroader* project layout.

The Woodland Scenics items can be limiting, with just two choices of grades and set heights for risers, but the method is a viable, light-weight alternative that will build into a strong layout.

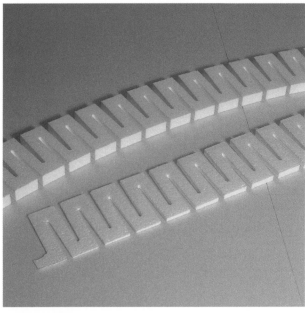

19 Woodland Scenics makes flexible foam grades and risers in several heights. These can be glued to a foam or wood base.

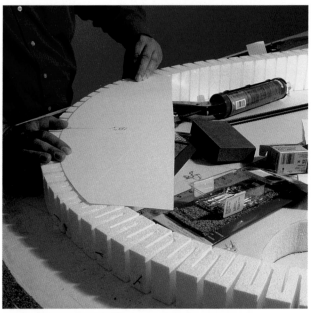

20 Use curve templates to determine the locations of the foam risers.

21 *Model Railroader's* Rock Ridge Central HO project layout used Woodland Scenics foam risers.

Small plywood frame table

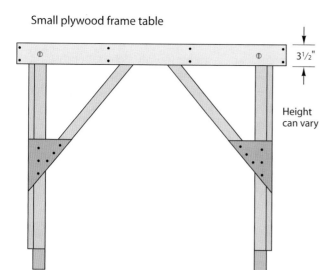

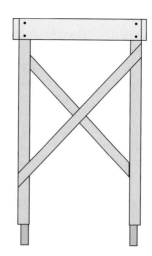

3½"

Height
can vary

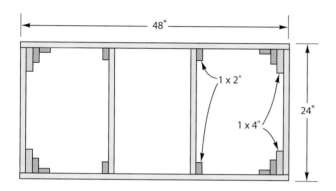

48"

24"

1 x 2"

1 x 4"

Plywood alternative

Use plywood strips in place of dimensional lumber

Finding straight dimensional lumber can be a challenge, and buying select or no. 1 boards can be prohibitively expensive. One way around that is to cut your own benchwork members from plywood.

Doing this is a bit of work, but because of plywood's excellent dimensional stability the result is boards that are straight and won't warp. This method can be used for large layouts (if you're willing to make a lot of sawdust) and also works well for small tables, modules, and sectional layouts.

The drawings above show the small (2 x 4-foot) table that I built.

The framing is made from 3½"-wide strips of ¾" plywood. You can use a similar design up to 4 x 8 feet; later in this chapter you'll find another slightly different design that works well for larger tables.

Start with a good flat sheet of plywood—¾" B-B (B-C if the C side is especially clean) pine or fir. Make sure the label reads "Group 1" lumber—this will be stronger than plywood made from group 2 wood.

A table saw is the easiest way to cut the plywood into strips. If you don't have a table saw, you can still get straight, true cuts using a circular saw. To do this, instead of trying to freehand the cuts, use a

Materials for 2 x 4-foot plywood table

Lumber	Hardware
¾" plywood, 2 x 4 feet, 1	¼" x 3" carriage bolts,
1 x 2, 8-foot, 2	nuts, and washers, 4
1 x 2, 1 x 4, scraps for	no. 8 x 1¾" screws, 16
corners	no. 8 x 1¼" screws, 8
¼" plywood, scraps for	no. 8 x ¾" screws, 24
gussets	T-nuts with threaded feet
	(optional), 4

straight board (I used the straightest 1 x 4 in my collection) as a fence for the saw.

Start by measuring the distance from the edge of the saw blade to the edge of the saw to determine the location for the fence (4½″ from the cut, in my case), as fig. 1 shows.

You can clamp the fence board in place, as fig. 2 shows, provided that the body of the saw will clear the clamp. Mine wouldn't, so I used drywall screws to secure the guide board to the plywood. Figure 3 shows how the saw follows the fence.

The table frame is similar to that of the butt-joint table in Chapter 2. However, I decided to use 1 x 2s at the corners to increase the strength of the joints, because screws driven into the ends of plywood have little strength. Glue the joint, then drive screws through the plywood into the corner pieces to secure them (figs. 5 and 6). Figure 7 shows the completed frame.

1 Measure the distance from the edge of the blade to the edge of the saw.

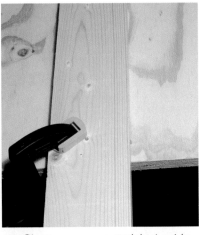

2 Clamp or screw a straight 1 x 4 in place to serve as a rip fence for the saw.

3 Guide the saw smoothly along the board.

4 Screw the joist to the 1 x 2.

5 Then drive screws through the side into the edge of the 1 x 2. The result is a very strong joint.

6 The completed frame is square and solid.

YOU HAVE TWO OPTIONS with the legs. If you want you can simply use stock 2 x 2s (or 2 x 4s for large tables), as with the tables in Chapters 2 and 3.

However, as long as you're ripping plywood into strips, you can use it to make legs as well. Joining two strips into an L results in extremely strong and stable legs.

I used 2¼″-wide strips for the legs, gluing them together to form an L as fig. 8 shows. Use 4d finishing nails to secure them until the glue dries.

Add a 6″ length of 2 x 2 at the base of the L, as fig. 9 shows. Glue it in place so that 4″ is in the leg L and 2″ extends from the L. Use drywall or wood screws to secure the 2 x 2.

Add a T-nut and leveling pad to the bottom of each leg, as in fig. 10. This is optional, but it will prove handy for leveling the legs on uneven floors.

Clamp the legs in place in each

7 Glue one edge of a leg piece, clamp the pieces together in an L, and use finishing nails to hold them together.

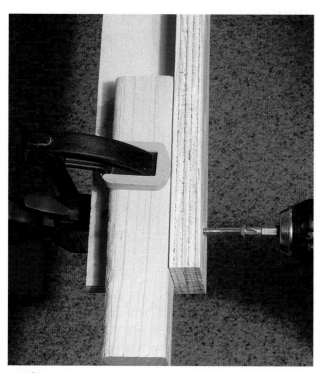

8 Glue and screw a length of 2 x 2 at the base of each leg.

9 Add a T-nut and leveler to each leg, as with the table in Chapter 2.

corner. See fig. 11. Make sure each leg is square to the frame, then drill a ¼″ hole through the side and leg and add a ¼″ carriage bolt, washer, and nut.

Add 1 x 2 cross bracing across the ends, as with other table designs. One 1 x 2 goes inside the L brackets (fig. 12); the other goes on the outside.

Figure 13 and the drawing in fig. 1 show how the side braces fit. For a free-standing table you should ideally fasten the braces as close to the bottom of the legs as possible. However, if you're planning to use the table as a module with other tables, the bracing shown should be sufficient. Figure 13 shows the finished table.

10 Clamp the legs in place, check them for square, and screw or bolt the legs to the frame.

11 Add one end brace inside the legs and one outside. The joint will be stronger if you start the screws on the plywood side of each.

12 The joint will be stronger if you start the screws on the plywood side of each.

13 The completed table shows both leg options: plywood Ls at one end and 2 x 2s at the other.

THE PLYWOOD FRAME technique works well for larger tables as well as small ones. *Model Railroader* senior editor Jim Hediger designed the portable table shown on page 41 for MR's 4 x 8-foot Rock Ridge Central project layout.

The basic construction is similar to that of the smaller table, but Jim used ½″ birch plywood ripped into 3″-wide strips. The resulting table is light but extremely strong.

The photos show the construction steps. No dimensions are given—you can adjust the height (or table size) to suit your needs.

Start by making the frame. Jim glued the butt joints with carpenter's glue, then used finishing nails to secure them. See fig. 14. You could do the same with the smaller table shown earlier, provided that you use a sheet of plywood for a tabletop. The finished frame is shown in fig. 15.

Run a bead of glue along the top of the frame pieces, then add the plywood top and use small trim nails to hold it in place. This layout uses ¼″ pine or fir plywood for the top, sufficient to support the foam scenery that was planned.

The legs are 3″-wide strips, but made just as the legs on the smaller table.

Figure 16 shows Jim adding the cross bracing, which is made from ¼″ x 1¼″ plain wood molding.

The bracing and legs are all secured with carriage bolts and wing nuts, making it an easy and quick process to disassemble and reassemble the table. That, combined with the table's light weight, make it an ideal design for a portable layout.

14 The completed frame is designed to be topped with thin plywood. You'd need to add additional cross members to support a cookie-cutter top or free-form subroadbed.

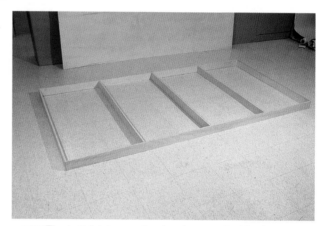

15 The butt joints are glued and secured with trim nails.

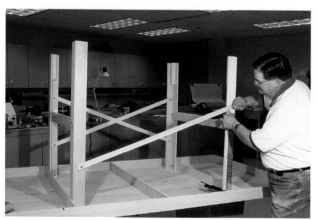

16 The cross bracing is ¼" x 1¼" plain molding.

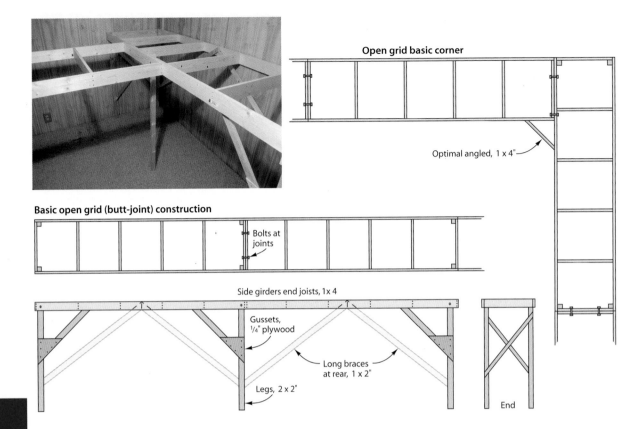

Open grid basic corner

Optimal angled, 1 x 4"

Basic open grid (butt-joint) construction

Bolts at joints

Side girders end joists, 1x 4

Gussets, ¼" plywood

Long braces at rear, 1 x 2"

Legs, 2 x 2"

End

Project Power Tools

Open-grid benchwork

Expanding benchwork around a room

Materials for open-grid benchwork, initial 30" x 8-foot section

Lumber	Hardware
1 x 4, 8-foot, 4	¼" x 3" carriage bolts, nuts, and washers, 4
2 x 2, 8-foot, 2	no. 8 x 1¾" screws, 64
1 x 2, 8-foot, 4	no. 8 x ¾" screws, 12
¼" plywood, scraps for gussets	T-nuts with threaded feet (optional), 4

Open-grid—also known as butt-joint—benchwork is an excellent choice for linear around-the-walls layouts, and it's also adaptable to odd-shaped areas. When you're designing benchwork, a good way to look at the open-grid style is as a series of interconnected boxes, each of which can be rectangular, square, or odd-shaped. Linking the boxes together provides a solid base for a layout.

The method is very versatile—once the grid is together, sub-roadbed, roads, rivers, and other elements can be added at various levels above and below the frame.

This chapter explains free-standing benchwork, which is solid and will still allow a great deal of open space below the layout for wiring access and storage.

Free-standing benchwork works well in basements where it would

be difficult or undesirable to anchor a layout to a concrete wall. It's also good to use in finished areas if you don't want to mar the surface of existing walls.

Free-standing open-grid construction is quite similar to the simple grid table in Chapter 2. Building a larger layout is a matter of expanding beyond the first table by adding a series of additional tables.

The drawings above show the basics of open-grid construction.

Each grid can be almost any size, but the practical limit on length is 8 feet. Longer tables would require additional (or inset) legs (as shown in Chapter 2).

Don't make tables any wider than a comfortable reach. If you're tall with a medium to fairly short (48" or lower) layout, 30" is well within reason; taller layouts greatly reduce the length of your reach.

START IN ONE CORNER with the first frame, then work outward from there. Make the grid itself in the same way as the frame for the table in Chapter 2. Add the end cross bracing as with the table (see fig. 1).

Figure 2 shows the completed first grid table. Note how the lengthwise bracing is longer at the rear than the front. This will provide a strong table and give you better under-table access for wiring and storage.

If you're planning to add a backdrop—which I highly recommend—you'll need to add vertical supports for it. I use 1 x 2s mounted every 48″, as fig. 3 shows. Add one mounting screw, then check with a level before adding a second screw.

The height of the supports will vary depending upon your layout and ceiling height. Cut and install them so their tops are about 2″ from the ceiling. Chapter 10 goes

1 Add cross bracing to each end of the first grid table

2 Note how the lengthwise braces are shorter at the front than at the rear.

3 Clamp the vertical 1 x 2 in place.

Use a level to make sure it is vertical.

Use two screws to secure each one.

into detail on installing the back-drop itself.

Add the second grid/table to the first. You need only two legs, since the first grid will support one end of the second. Clamp the two together to get proper alignment, then use ¼" carriage or hex bolts to attach them as in fig. 4. Use two bolts for narrow (24" or less) joining faces; use a bolt at each end and every 15" or so for wider faces.

Add a long brace from the rear leg of the first table to the mid-point of the second frame as fig. 5 shows, and add cross bracing to the two legs of the second grid. Locking several grids together like this will result in a very strong, sturdy layout.

Figure 6 and the drawings on page 46 show how to join two grids in a corner. After bolting them together and adding the long rear brace, add a 45-degree brace from

the leg to the grid by the inside corner. This strengthens the joint.

Adding a peninsula is similar. Just bolt the first grid of the peninsula to the grid of the main layout, as fig. 7 shows. If this junction is near the middle of the main layout grid you may have to add a single leg, as the photo shows. The drawing in fig. 8 shows how you can make the end of a peninsula wide to provide for a turnback curve.

You're not limited to square cor-

4 Clamp the second grid frame to the first, then use carriage bolts to connect them. Tighten the bolts securely with a socket or wrench.

5 Add a 1 x 2 brace from the rear leg of the first table to the midpoint of the second grid.

6 A diagonal brace from the inside of the corner joint down to the leg will strengthen the joint.

ners. Adding 1 x 4 fillers at grid joints makes the benchwork flow more smoothly and adds valuable space to the layout. Figure 9 shows how to add these pieces. It's easy to round these corners later using fascia, as shown in Chapter 10.

You're not limited to 45-degree angles—the drawings in fig. 10 show how these can be used with grids of various shapes and sizes. Note how side girders need not be parallel (a miter saw is vital in cutting these odd-angled joists).

Figure 10 also shows how you can get around furnaces and other obstacles. Doing this is just a matter of putting the grid pieces together and using some creativity, as the benchwork in fig. 11 shows.

If you have enough room and enough helpers, you can also put together a fairly large grid before adding legs.

Now that the benchwork is in place, turn to Chapter 7 to learn the basics of free-form subroadbed on risers.

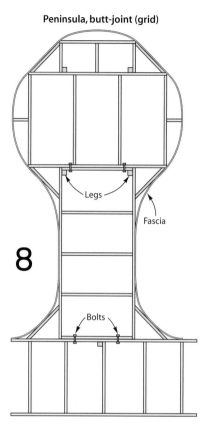

Peninsula, butt-joint (grid)

Legs

Fascia

8

Bolts

7 If you add a peninsula at the middle of another table, you'll have to add a leg for support.

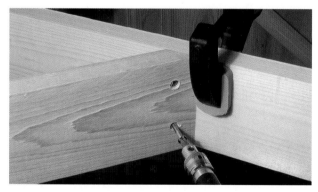

9 Use a miter saw to cut a 1 x 4 to fit the corner. Clamp the piece in place, then drill pilot holes at each end and screw it in place.

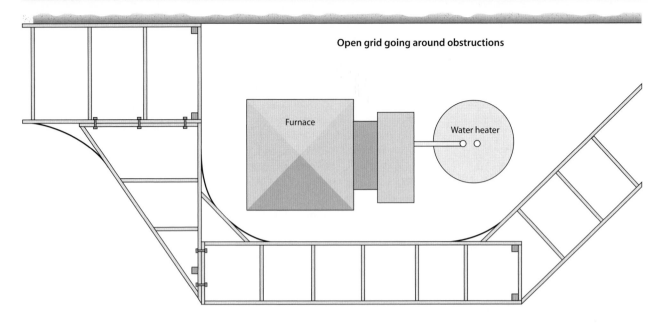

Open grid going around obstructions

Furnace

Water heater

10

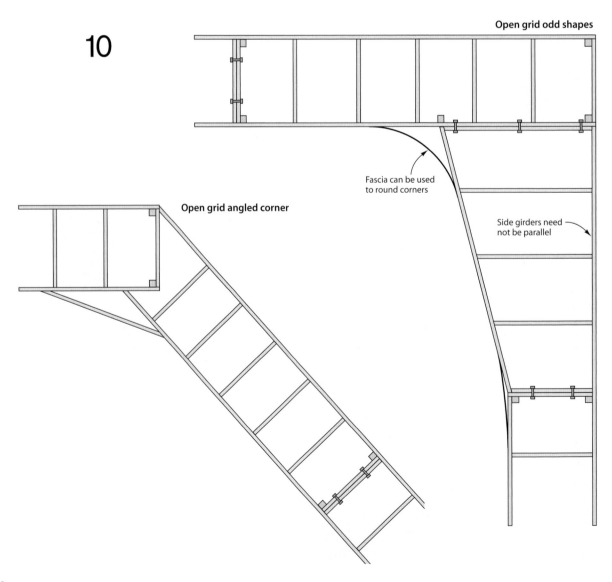

Open grid odd shapes

Fascia can be used
to round corners

Side girders need
not be parallel

Open grid angled corner

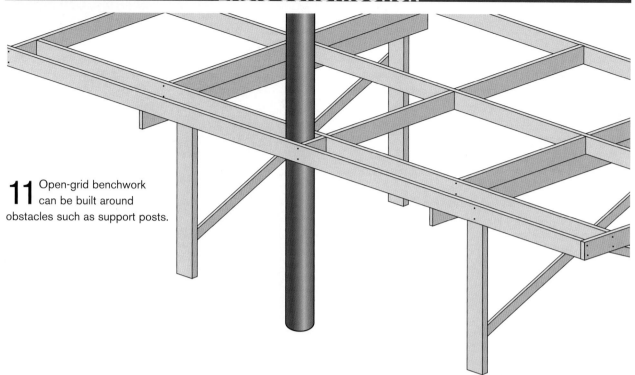

11 Open-grid benchwork can be built around obstacles such as support posts.

Modular and sectional benchwork

Although modular and sectional layouts are both designed to be moved, it's important to know that there's a difference: *Modular* and *sectional* are not the same thing, and the terms aren't interchangeable.

Modular means that each section is built to the same overall specifications, so each can be swapped or interchanged with another one. For example, a 4-foot Ntrak module can be taken out of a layout, and virtually any other one can be substituted in its place.

Sectional means that a layout can be disassembled into pieces, but each section is not necessarily interchangeable with the others. Sections may be different shapes and sizes with varied track arrangements.

Modular and sectional model railroading has grown in popularity over the past 25 years. The driving force in modular design has been Ntrak, the group that has established widely accepted standards for N scale.

For home and club layouts, sectional construction can offer some advantages over permanent benchwork.

Let's look at modules first.

Modular model railroading

The basic premise of modular railroading is that anyone can build a module that matches a group's standards and then at any time meet with other members of the group to join their modules together. The success of Ntrak has shown this to be a popular option.

Some choose to build a module because they don't have room for a larger layout. Others might build a single module but integrate it into a larger permanent layout.

The drawing shows dimensions and specifications for Ntrak's standard 4-foot module; Ntrak offers several other options as well. The photo shows a 4-foot Ntrak module. Modules can be built in

CONTINUED ON PAGE 52

Ntrak modules must follow certain specifications, but the scenery can vary from mountains to prairies to cities.

Ray and Renee Grosser built their HO Soo Line layout in sections to enable them to take it to shows across the country.

CONTINUED FROM PAGE 51

6- and 8-foot lengths, as well as inside and outside corner modules.

Many clubs and smaller groups have also come up with their own modular designs. Modular design is wise for portable club layouts. That way, if a member or two can't make it to the show with his modules, the remaining modules can still be rearranged to make a smaller layout.

Here are a few things to remember when designing and building a module or series of modules:

• Each module should stand by itself, with its own set of legs, and each leg should have adjustable feet.

• Electrical connections between modules should be via plugs and sockets to make for easy connections. Each set of electrical wires (track power, signals, switch machines, etc.) should have a unique plug/socket design.

• Turnouts and curved track should be avoided above section/module joints.

Sectional layouts

Most sectional layouts fall into two categories: Those that are designed to be moved often, such as a club or individual who brings a layout to shows, and those designed to be moved once, such as when the modeler is buying a new home.

If you have a layout that fits the first category, build it using the key points listed above with modular layouts. Ray and Renee Grosser's Soo Line layout is an example.

David Barrow has rebuilt his HO Cat Mountain & Santa Fe layout in what he calls "dominoes," to make it easier for him to rearrange and change the layout plan.

It's extremely rare for a layout to survive a move unless it has been designed to move in the first place. Many modelers consider a move as a chance to start fresh in a new space, but if you want to move your layout, design it that way from the start.

Butt-joint construction is usually the method of choice for sections and modules, because the design results in flush vertical mating faces on all four sides of each module.

A couple of factors to keep in mind:

• The space that you're moving to might not match the existing space well enough to use all of the sections. This might still be okay if you can use the sections with minor modifications, or if you can use most of your existing sections.

• Keep the size of each section manageable. Not only must you be able to get it out of its current location, you must make sure that it's small enough to get into its next home. Don't consider just table size—hills and other scenic details can add several inches, and you'll want a few inches of space all around to minimize the chances of dinging the layout when moving. Eight feet is quite long—4 to 6 feet is much more manageable, with a 2-foot width.

• Use terminal strips or other connectors to make electrical connections between sections. Label all connections and wires upon initial installation.

• Provide a positive alignment mechanism between sections. Carriage bolts are one method. Hinge plates and pins are another, as the photo shows.

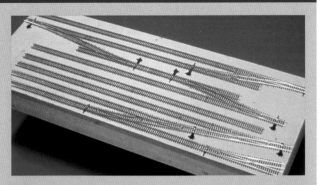

David Barrow built his HO layout using a series of sections that he calls "dominoes."

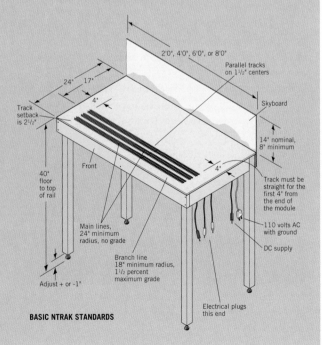

Door hinge plates and pins can be used to lock sections or modules together.

BASIC NTRAK STANDARDS

Access hatches

If you have a wide table or deep shelf on your layout, creating areas that are beyond a comfortable reach, you need to provide access to that area. The most common way to do this is with a hidden access panel.

As with lift-out track sections (Chapter 11) it's best to keep them as simple as possible. Start by framing an opening in your benchwork and cutting a panel (a piece of plywood is fine) that drops into place. When building scenery, continue the scenery across the access panel.

The size can vary, but make sure the opening is large enough to fit through to do routine maintenance (such as cleaning track and scenery or rerailing trains).

The photos show how a cattle pen fits into an opening on David Haines' N scale layout. Although David didn't design this as an access panel, it's a perfect illustration of how to build one (although it would need to be larger).

You can also build access panels in mountainous areas, as the photo shows, but construction becomes more complex.

Although not an access panel, this removable scene illustrates a great way to make one. Start by framing an opening. Note the wooden stops partially in the opening that keep the cattle pen (on a piece of plywood) from falling through.

Access panels can also be located in hills or mountains. Be sure the opening is large enough for you to fit through.

Creative Solutions

Sometimes you have to get really creative when designing layouts and benchwork, as this model railroader did on his HO layout. He needed to connect a staging yard with one end of his railroad, but the stairs were in his way. His solution? Simply run the track across one of the stair treads. As long as the rails are depressed below tread level, they won't be damaged by people walking up the steps, although people must be alert for a real railroad crossing!

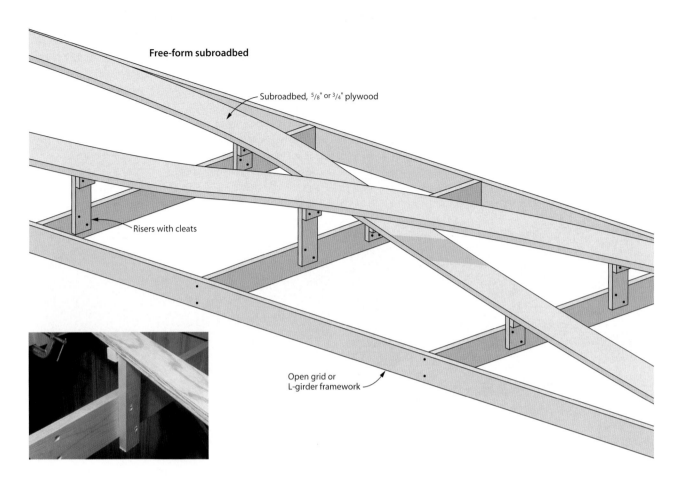

Free-form subroadbed

Subroadbed, ⅝" or ¾" plywood

Risers with cleats

Open grid or
L-girder framework

Free-form subroadbed

The secrets of roadbed, risers, and cleats

Free-flowing subroadbed can be used above either open-grid or L-girder benchwork. It's among the most common techniques used on medium- and large-sized layouts. The drawing in fig. 1 shows the basic idea.

This method is related to the cookie-cutter method shown in Chapter 4, and some modelers use cookie-cutter subroadbed on large layouts. However, unless you're modeling the prairie or a big city where you need the large flat surface, doing so usually isn't an economical use of plywood. You can still use smaller pieces of plywood under areas such as towns, individual structures, rivers, and roads.

Plywood is the material of choice for subroadbed. It's strong, dimensionally stable, and economical—you can get a great deal of subroadbed from a single 4 x 8 sheet.

The narrower plywood is cut, the weaker it becomes. I've had good luck with ⅝" A-C or B-C plywood, but some modelers prefer the extra strength of ¾". Whichever you choose, when shopping for plywood, check the stamp as described in Chapter 1—always buy the stronger Group 1 plywood if possible.

START BY MAKING a full-size drawing of your track plan. I like to get the plan onto paper, full-size on the benchwork. (Another—in many ways easier—method is to do it on the floor before beginning benchwork assembly.)

You can often get large sheets or rolls of blank newsprint, or you can do as I did and buy a roll of brown wrapping paper. It's inexpensive and very handy, as it comes in 24″-wide rolls in 50- and 100-foot lengths.

Use a pencil to rough in the track plan. I like to use plastic templates that I made (see the sidebar on page 56) for roughing in the curves. For sharper curves you can use a yardstick as a compass, as shown in Chapter 4. For straight track, 3-and 4-foot aluminum rulers are handy, and for long straightaways use the straightest 1 x 2 you can find.

Once you have drawn the plan on the paper, measure and mark the width that the subroadbed needs to be. This will vary depending upon your scale, the type of roadbed you plan to use, and how much of a shoulder you desire. About 2½″ is typical for HO scale.

As you're drawing the subroadbed outline, be sure to mark areas where you need to leave the surface wider for cities and other areas. Also mark the location of joists and joints between grid sections, as fig. 1 shows.

If you have any hidden track, be sure to add that as well. The sidebar on page 56 provides a couple of ideas for planning and adding hidden track.

Cut out the paper following the outlines of the subroadbed and other features. See fig. 2. The pieces will serve as templates in cutting out the plywood. Label the pieces of paper so that you'll be able to arrange the finished pieces properly once they're cut from the plywood.

Place the paper templates on the plywood. Since an 8-foot run is the best you can get from a sheet of plywood, you'll have to cut the subroadbed templates in places. Avoid making these cuts within 5″ of the marks indicating joists and grid joints. Position the templates to get the most subroadbed out of the wood with the least amount of waste.

Tape the templates down as in fig. 3 and use a pencil or marker to outline them. Be sure to label them to make it easier to get them on the layout in the proper order. The photo also shows how to use photocopies of turnouts to ensure that the space will work out.

Mark the turnout locations on the plywood to make it easier to place them later. I mark the throw bar location with a scriber, as fig. 4 shows.

Use a saber saw to cut out the subroadbed sections, then position the sections atop the grid.

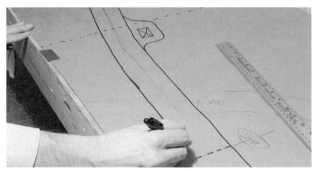

1 Pencil in the track center lines and other features such as roads. Use a felt-tip marker to indicate cut lines and mark joist locations.

2 Cut out the paper templates with a hobby or utility knife.

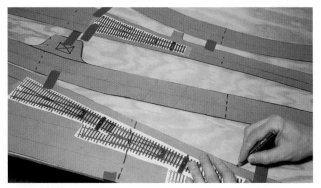

3 Tape the strips of cut-out paper to the plywood and outline them in pencil, then marker. Photocopies of turnouts ensure that you allow enough room for them on the subroadbed.

4 Mark turnout locations on the plywood by using a scriber to poke an indentation at throw bar locations.

Curve templates

Templates make it easy to draw broad curves in full size. You can set them on top of the benchwork and get a good idea of the space taken up by a curve of a particular radius. When you're drawing full-size plans they ensure accurate measurements.

I made my templates from large pieces of .060" styrene that I had handy (you can buy styrene in 4 x 8-foot sheets from plastics dealers in most medium-size and larger cities—check the Yellow Pages), but you can also use hardboard or thin plywood. Cardboard also works, but isn't nearly as durable.

To make a template, use a 1 x 2 or other long stick as a compass. Use a piece of plywood as a table. Tack one end of the stick to the plywood and draw an arc at the desired radius on the styrene (you can have a different radius on each edge of each template, as the photo shows). Cut out the template, and it's ready to use.

My templates are each about 40" long. That seems to be a

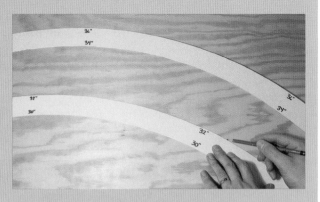

good length: Any longer and they become awkward to use; if they're shorter it's difficult to lay out and judge long curves.

I made a set in even-number increments from 22" to 50" and find that I've used just about all of them.

Hidden track

Many times a track plan will require hidden hidden track, usually along the rear of a layout. These photos show one way of hiding track. The hidden track travels at the rear of the shelf, at joist level near the backdrop. A track on risers is in front of it, and the hidden track will be covered by scenery extending from the rear of the visible track to the backdrop.

If you have hidden track extending to a lower level, you can notch joists or cut specially shaped joists to allow the track to pass through. The diagrams on page 59 show several options for both butt-joint and L-girder benchwork.

Whenever you have hidden track, take precautions to make sure that a derailment doesn't turn into a major disaster with trains hitting the floor. You can make small fences from hardboard as the photo shows and screw them into place on the sides. You want the fences tall enough that they contain derailed equipment, but not so tall that you can't reach over to fix any problems.

One method of hiding track is to run it at the rear of the layout at a lower level than the main track.

Use fences on any track standing alone below scenery level to keep trains from hitting the floor.

CHANGING ELEVATION IS a matter of using risers. It's a good idea to use risers even if you don't plan to have any grades on your trackwork. Doing so makes it easy to keep the track above the base scenery. It will also be easier to add scenic details such as lakes and rivers below track level.

Figure 5 shows a typical riser assembly. Note how the risers are attached to 1 x 1 cleats, with a screw from under the cleat into the subroadbed.

This keeps screwheads from interfering with the roadbed and makes it easy to move a riser if it becomes necessary (which

happens more often than one might think).

A 1 x 2 is usually sufficient for a riser. Cut the cleats as wide as the subroadbed, or a bit wider—they can always be cut off later.

Attach the cleat to the riser with a pair of screws (drill countersunk holes first) as fig. 6 shows, but first

Riser construction

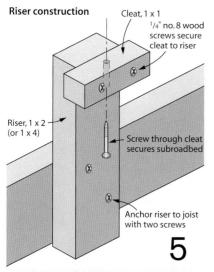

Cleat, 1 x 1

¹/₄" no. 8 wood screws secure cleat to riser

Riser, 1 x 2 (or 1 x 4)

Screw through cleat secures subroadbed

Anchor riser to joist with two screws

5

6 Attach the cleat to the riser with a pair of screws in countersunk holes.

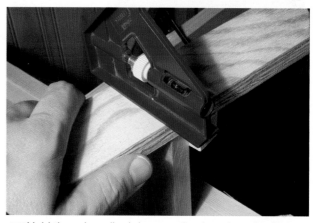

7 Hold the subroadbed down on the riser, then check to make sure the subroadbed is level across the riser.

8 Clamp the risers in place, checking that the subroadbed is level or at the proper grade.

drill the center pilot hole for mounting to the subroadbed. Drill this hole at a slight angle away from the riser to make it easier to get the screw bit in the space.

Begin installation by clamping a riser in place at the highest elevation. Make sure that the riser is level across the subroadbed, as fig. 7 shows. Install a riser at a lower level, then add the risers in between, clamping (not screwing) the

risers in place as you go. See fig. 8.

A carpenter's level with markings is a handy tool for calculating grades. See the sidebar on page 59 for details on making one.

Once you're sure that a series of risers are in the proper place, you can mount each to the joists with a pair of screws, as in fig. 9. Add a screw from under the cleat to secure the subroadbed, as fig. 10 shows.

You can get creative in installing risers. Complex benchwork may require some unorthodox mounting methods, so it's good to keep in mind that risers don't necessarily have to be attached directly under the track they support.

The drawings in fig. 11 show several alternate mounting methods, and fig. 12 shows one way of extending a riser.

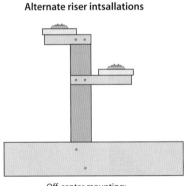

9 Keep the clamp in place as you secure each riser with a pair of screws.

10 Drive a screw through the cleat into the plywood to secure it.

Alternate riser intsallations

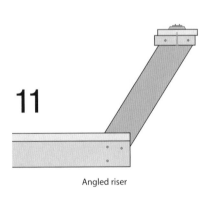

11

Angled riser

Off-center mounting; multiple supports on one riser

Multiple routes on one riser

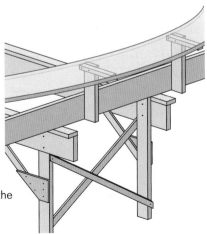

12 Here's one way to extend the reach of a riser.

Options for track below joist level

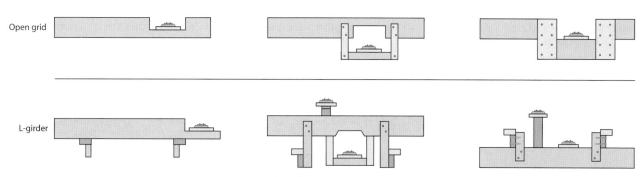

Open grid

L-girder

Grade gauge

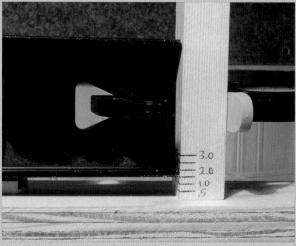

Here's a handy tool for helping you determine grades as you're installing subroadbed.

The grade–measured in percentages, as in 1 percent or 2.5 percent–is simply a measure of how much the roadbed rises or drops compared to the length of the run. A 1 percent grade rises one unit for every 100 units of run–for example, 1 inch for every 100 inches. Calculate the grade by dividing the rise by the run (in the above, $1 \div 100 = .01$, or 1 percent). Odd numbers are easy to calculate: For example, a rise of 2.5 inches in 130 inches would be 1.9 percent ($2.5 \div 130 = .019$).

Calculating the grade has nothing to do with scale. The grade is figured the same way on the prototype as a model (although the units of measure are often different).

To make a grade gauge, take a standard carpenter's level and clamp a stick to one end. Mark the stick in increments from the bottom end, and label them to indicate the grade. The chart below shows where to place the markings, depending upon the length of your level. The photo shows a 24" level, but 12" or 36" levels can also be handy, depending upon the size of your benchwork.

Grade Percentage	Length of level		
	12"	24"	36"
0.5 percent	.06"	.12"	.18"
1.0 percent	.12"	.24"	.36"
1.5 percent	.18"	.36"	.54"
2.0 percent	.24"	.48"	.72"
2.5 percent	.30"	.60"	.90"
3.0 percent	.36"	.72"	1.08"
3.5 percent	.42"	.84"	1.26"
4.0 percent	.48"	.96"	1.44"

FIGURE 13 SHOWS a joint in the subroadbed. Join the two pieces before anchoring the second piece of subroadbed to any risers.

Make a splice plate of at least ½" plywood (in this case I used ⅜").

See fig. 14. A good rule of thumb is to make the splice plate four times as long as the subroadbed is wide, with a 12" maximum.

Spread carpenter's yellow glue on the splice plate, then clamp it in

place. Drive at least four screws in place on each side of the splice.

The thickness of a plywood sheet can vary a bit, so every once in a while you'll have a joint where one piece is slightly thinner, as fig.

13 Try to arrange subroadbed pieces so that joints occur between risers.

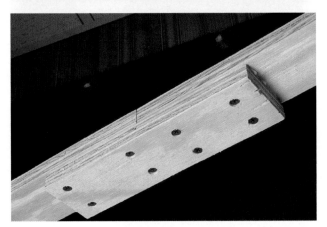

14 Glue and screw the splice plate in place, making sure that the two sections of subroadbed are in proper alignment.

15 shows. If this happens, use a Stanley Surform tool to shave down the high piece.

You can handle wide areas requiring support (such as yards and towns) by using a pair of 1 x 2 or 1 x 4 risers spread apart with a 1 x 2 horizontal member between them. See fig. 16.

As track curves, especially around corners, you'll find that you need to add additional supports.

Figure 17 shows one such area.

To fix this, position the new joist so that it falls at the midpoint of the subroadbed section that needs support. See fig. 18. If you're adding a joist at an angle, hold the

15 If one piece of plywood is slightly thicker than the other, shave it down with a plane or Surform tool.

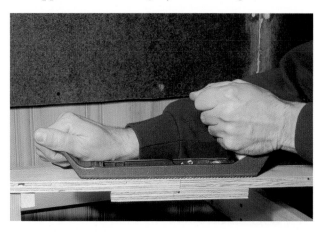

16 Support wide areas with a pair of risers connected by a 1 x 2.

17 If the distance between risers exceeds 16" or so, adding an additional joist and riser is a good idea.

new 1 x 4 under the grid and mark it with a pencil. Cut the joist using a miter saw, then install it. Add the new riser, and that section is complete.

There are many other ways to position and cut joists to allow for track on lower levels or other special situations. See the roadbed sidebar for a few ideas.

Congratulations—you're now ready to add roadbed. The sidebar on page 63 looks at several roadbed options available.

Turn to Chapter 10 for details on adding backdrops and fascia, two very important elements for giving your layout a clean, finished look.

18 Cut a new joist to fit, at an angle if necessary, then add the new riser.

Roadbed

This chapter explains how to get a firm, smooth, level sub-roadbed. The next step is to add roadbed that will give your track a similar smooth, level, seamless bed to lie on. Several materials will work well—here's a look at four of the most popular options:

• **Cork**—Cork was among the first widely available roadbed materials, and has been the hobby standard for many years. It comes in 36"-long strips perforated at an angle down the middle. Peeling it apart provides two matching beveled halves. It's made in most scales from N to O.

Cork is flexible, making it easy to lay around curves. It's easy to cut with a hobby or utility knife, making it easy to form bases for turnouts, although commercial turnout-shaped pads are made by Midwest and IBL.

There's usually a rough burr along the top of the beveled edges—use a sanding block and coarse sandpaper to get rid of this.

• **Homasote**—This dense fiber material holds spikes and track nails well, and it is regarded as the best choice for handlaying track. You can cut your own Homasote roadbed from sheets, but it can be difficult to find. Call the Homasote Corp. at 800-257-9491 to locate a dealer.

Another option—shown in the photos—is a product called Homabed, made by California Roadbed Co. Standard Homabed comes in strips with one edge beveled, like cork, but it isn't flexible. The company offers strips with kerfs cut along one edge, allowing it to curve. It also sells flat sheets for cutting into turnout pads.

• **Track-Bed**—This is a fairly new product from Woodland Scenics. It is a low-density foam product that comes as one piece (either 24" strips or a continuous roll) with beveled edges. It is quite flexible, and it's the softest of the roadbed materials.

• **Vinylbed**—This is a dense, flexible vinyl material that comes in 36" lengths precut with beveled edges. It easily bends around curves down to 15" radius (and can go tighter). An advantage is that it's available in a variety of widths and thicknesses, and subroadbed is also available in various profiles. It's made by Hobby Innovations.

Securing roadbed

All of the above materials are best glued in place. Use white glue, except when gluing Track-Bed to foam, in which case you can use Woodland Scenics Foam Tack Glue.

For all but Homasote you can use map pins or push pins to hold the roadbed pieces in place until the glue sets. For Homasote, either hold it down with pieces of strip lumber with weights on top or clamp it to the subroadbed.

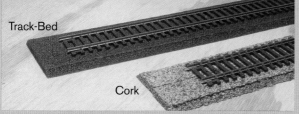

Track-Bed

Cork

Vinylbed

Homabed

Cork comes in a single piece perforated at an angle down the middle. Peeling the strips apart gives you matching beveled halves.

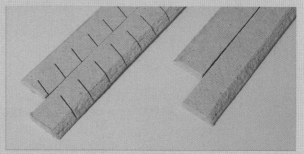

Homabed is precut with a bevel on one edge. Pieces are available cut with kerfs, allowing them to be curved.

Wall-mounted benchwork

Create more storage space . . .

8

**Project
Power
Tools**

Mounting benchwork directly to walls offers many advantages over free-standing layouts: Wall mounting allows you to get rid of many (sometimes all) legs, freeing the space under a layout for storage. Wall-mounted layouts are solid and they look neat, as they allow a layout to naturally conform to the shape of the space available.

You can wall-mount a layout in a finished room as well as on a bare concrete or concrete block wall. The keys to either are anchoring the benchwork firmly.

You can design wall-mounted benchwork based on L-girder or open-grid (butt-joint) styles, or a mixture of both. Once the framing is in place, the basic techniques are the same. We'll start by showing how to mount a layout to a finished wall.

PROBABLY THE SIMPLEST style of wall-mounted benchwork on a finished or stud wall, especially for an around-the-walls layout, is open-grid. Start by making the framework as shown in Chapter 6. As with a free-standing open-grid layout, the goal is to design the layout in a series of rectangles and boxes.

Once the frames are built, anchor the wall side of each frame directly to the wall as in fig. 1. The key is to use screws long enough that at least 1½″ of each extends into the stud. In my case I needed to pass through the ¾″ frame, ¼″ paneling, and ½″ drywall.

I used 3″ stainless-steel deck screws with square-drive heads. At first glance they look like silver drywall screws, but deck screws are much stronger than standard wood screws and have coarse threads that hold extremely well.

Clamp temporary legs in place to hold the frames at the proper height against the wall. Drive two deck screws through the frame into the wall at each stud location.

Figure 2 shows how I used 1 x 4 spacers to fill gaps at the end of a grid section. I had to do this to keep the grid off the corner trim.

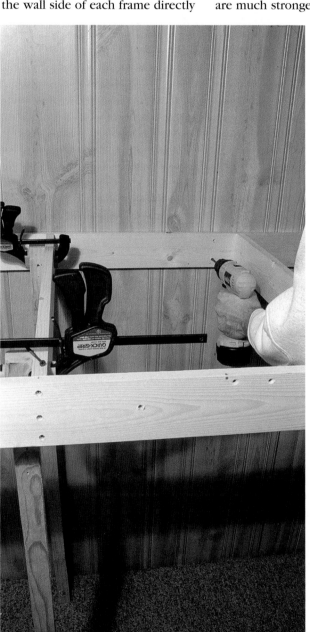

1 Clamp temporary legs in place to hold the frame at the proper height, then drill pilot holes in the frame and drive screws into the wall studs.

2 You may need to add spacer blocks behind some frames, as with this one to clear corner molding.

3 The first frame is solidly mounted to two walls.

Shim

4 If your room corners aren't quite square, you may have to add shims behind one side of the frame.

Figure 3 shows the first frame installed in a corner. If your room isn't quite square, you may have to use shims between the grid and wall. See fig. 4.

Continue adding frames from there, butting the second frame to the first, as in fig. 5. As with free-standing open-grid bench-

work, join the frames with bolts.

You have two bracing/leg options with this style of bench-work. You can simply use legs, or you can use diagonal braces to the wall. If you choose legs, a 2 x 2 will work fine. Use a carriage bolt to secure it to the frame at a corner, as fig. 6 shows.

Figure 7 shows a diagonal brace. Screw the bottom of the brace to a 6″ length of 2 x 2 that's anchored to a stud.

A leg or brace at each joint should be sufficient. Continue building the benchwork as you would for a free-standing layout.

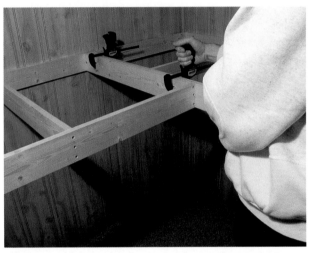

5 Clamp the second frame to the first, making sure that both are level. Join the two using carriage or hex bolts.

6 You can support the room side of this style of layout by adding a 2 x 2 leg at each joint between frames.

7 Another option is to add a diagonal brace from the wall to the frame. A short length of 2 x 2 screwed to a stud gives the brace a solid anchor at bottom.

THE METHODS SHOWN here work well for layouts from 18″ to about 36″ wide. For shelves under 18″ full-blown benchwork is overkill; instead, consider making simple shelves, as shown in Chapter 9. The shelves shown there are used as second decks, but they work fine for narrow single-level layouts.

The bracket design shown in fig. 8 can be adjusted for various widths. The key is that the bracket arm length shouldn't exceed 1.5 times its height. In other words, a 30″ bracket should be at least 45″ above the floor for the angle brace to do its job.

Once the wall anchors are in place, the actual benchwork (or table) for the layout isn't much different than the table-style benchwork discussed in earlier chapters.

This method works well on finished walls, and it's ideal for basement (concrete or block) walls as well. The sidebar on page 71 shows a couple of ways to prepare

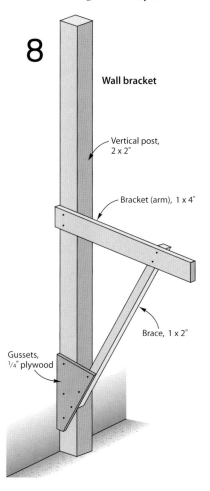

8

Wall bracket

Vertical post, 2 x 2″

Bracket (arm), 1 x 4″

Brace, 1 x 2″

Gussets, ¼″ plywood

9 Anchor 2 x 2s to the walls using screws long enough to securely grab the wall studs.

10 Add one screw to hold the bracket, then make sure that it's level before driving the second screw into place.

a basement wall for wall-mounted benchwork.

Start by installing vertical 2 x 2s, as fig. 9 shows. Having them every 24″ to 32″ is sufficient; if you're installing them in a finished room, you'll be limited by locations of the wall studs. Be SURE that you anchor them to a stud, or the 2 x 2 will have no strength and will eventually pull away from the wall.

For the finished walls I used the same 3″ deck screws as when anchoring the open-grid bench-work; no. 10 wood screws are also a good choice. Use at least four screws in each 2 x 2: One at the top and bottom, one at the approximate layout/bracket height, and one about 12″ above the bracket height (or at the second-deck height, if you're planning one).

Install the horizontal 1 x 4 brackets as fig. 10 shows. Clamp the bracket into place, drive one 2″ no. 8 screw to hold it, then use a level to make sure the bracket is horizontal before driving the second screw into place.

You may have to get creative in

11 Stud placement dictates where the brackets are located, so creativity is often required in corners.

12 Secure the diagonal 1 x 2 brace to the 2 x 2 with a ¼″ plywood gusset plate.

corners, depending upon the stud location. Figure 11 shows how I joined one wall bracket to the first bracket on the adjoining wall.

Add 1 x 2 angle braces from the base of the wall to each bracket. Make sure that the brace won't interfere with the L-girder when it's installed. Cut the brace to fit, clamp the brace at the top, and use a gusset plate to secure the bottom, as fig. 12 shows.

Screw the top of the brace to the bracket, checking the bracket with a level, as in fig. 13. Figure 14 shows several brackets installed.

Make the L-girders as described in Chapter 3. With brackets set this close together, using 1 x 2s for both web and flange is sufficient.

Clamp the girders in place under the brackets, as fig. 15 shows. The flange should face the room on both girders to provide easier access for screwing joists in place.

Remember the rule of fifths—each girder should be located ⅕ of the way in from each end. Screw the girders to the brackets from below. Since the girders are

13 Make sure the bracket is level before screwing the diagonal brace into place.

14 Here's the room with several bracket assemblies in place.

15 Screw the L-girders in place under the brackets using long wood screws. Make sure the flange faces the room.

16 Screwing a short 2 x 2 to the girder and bracket strengthens the joint.

hanging from the brackets, use long screws—at least 1¾″ or 2″ no. 8 wood screws.

To add stability and strength at the bracket joints, add additional 2 x 2 braces at every other bracket, as shown in fig. 16.

Figure 17 shows how to join L-girders at corners. Notch the flange on the girder that is perpendicular to the first girder. Add a screw through the web of the first girder to lock the girders together. You can position the joists as desired on the corner area as fig. 18 shows.

Figure 19 shows the completed wall brackets and girders in place.

You can see how wide open it is under this 24″-wide layout.

If you plan to add a backdrop, add horizontal 1 x 2 strips above the bracket arms and at the top of the 2 x 2s, as fig. 20 shows. Chapter 10 explains how to install a backdrop.

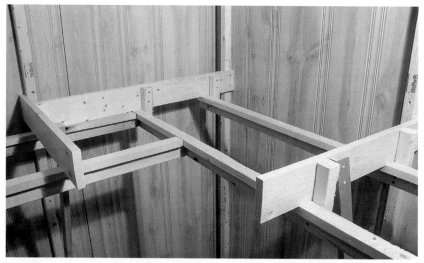

17 Notch the flanges on the girders that are perpendicular to the original girder, then add a screw to each to secure them.

18 Joists can be positioned at almost any angle around the corner.

19 This style of benchwork results in a wide-open area underneath the layout.

20 Add horizontal 1 x 2s across the 2 x 2s as backdrop supports.

Wall mounting with concrete and block walls

The first step is to provide a surface on the wall to which you can anchor the layout. A series of 2 x 2s will provide good strength, just as on a finished wall earlier in this chapter.

Use masonry screws and anchors to secure the 2 x 2 to the wall. Determine the heights you'll need the anchors, just as with a finished wall. Use a masonry bit to drill holes in the mortar lines (for concrete block walls) or directly into the wall (for a poured concrete wall).

Tap masonry anchors into place in each hole. Drill screw clearance holes in the 2 x 2 to match the anchor locations, then drive the screws into place. Use at least a no. 10 screw (with anchors sized to match), and make sure the screws are long enough to go all the way into the anchors.

The advantage in this technique is that you can locate the 2 x 2s wherever you need them. Usually a 24" to 36" spacing is sufficient.

Framing a wall

Another method is to frame the entire wall, as shown in the photo at lower left. (you can also see this in fig. 23). Doing this takes a bit more wood than the first technique, but has the advantage that you (or a subsequent owner) can use the studs to finish the walls.

Anchor the top plate (horizontal 2 x 4) to the underside of the joists. The footer (bottom horizontal 2 x 4) can be glued to the floor with construction adhesive. It's a good idea to use treated lumber for the footer to combat potential moisture problems.

Many home improvement guides offer detailed information on framing basement walls.

WHEN MARK WATSON planned his N scale layout, he decided to use wall-mounted brackets with butt-joint boxes sitting on top of the brackets. He later built scenery based on layers of foam above the plywood top.

Mark made his brackets as fig. 21 shows. To do this, make a miter cut on the 1 x 4 brace, then use prefab metal nailing strips (on both sides) to fasten the brace to the 1 x 4 bracket. The free ends of each are screwed to wall studs.

The grid sections are made in the same way as other butt-joint frames, as a series of boxes made from 1 x 4s. The frames are secured to the brackets with short boards screwed to both bracket and frame, as in fig. 22.

Figure 23 shows the completed sections in place, including their ¼" plywood tops.

21 Mark Watson secured the arms and braces of his brackets with metal nailing strips.

22 The wall brackets hold a series of frames made from 1 x 4s. Short lengths of 1 x 2s and 2 x 2s hold the frames to the brackets.

23 Mark covered the frames with thin plywood to support foam scenery.

Double-deck benchwork

Double up your layout space

9

Probably the biggest reason modelers choose multiple-deck layouts is to get more railroading out of a given space. Adding a second deck can dramatically increase the layout area, in some cases making it possible to nearly double the length of a main line.

Although some layouts are completely double-decked, a much more common method is to double-deck only part of a railroad. The extra deck (upper or lower) can be a branch line, staging area, industry, or separate railroad. In the case of staging, the second deck is often hidden from sight on a lower level.

Another possibility is to have the added deck completely separate from the main deck. Each level can then be its own layout, with a different scale or theme on each.

Before planning an extensive multiple-deck layout, consider the disadvantages to double-deck layouts. The first is increased construction complexity. Viewing angles are also a concern—adding a second level often means that neither level ends up at the optimum viewing height.

There's also a limited height to each deck. This isn't much of a problem if you're modeling the prairie, but it can be quite limiting if you're modeling a mountain railroad or a large city with tall buildings.

Another potential problem is getting trains to the second level. Figure 1 shows a couple ways of doing this. One method with a point-to-point layout is to start it along one wall, then have it climb as it circles the room, becoming the upper deck when it completes the circuit.

Another way to reach the second level is to branch off the main loop and have the branch climb on scenery until it reaches the height of the upper deck.

Helixes have long been used, but they require a tremendous amount of space. Figure 2 shows a fairly simple one-loop helix; to gain more height, a helix can make multiple turns, as fig. 3 shows.

A good rule of thumb is to keep the upper deck at or less than two-thirds the depth of the main level. This isn't an absolute rule, but doing so provides better access to the rear of the main level and less of a reach to the upper level.

Lighting is another reason. By following the two-thirds rule, enough light will usually reach the rear areas of the main deck. If the upper deck is as wide as the lower, it usually becomes necessary to provide additional lighting beneath the deck to light the lower level.

1

Partially double-decked layouts

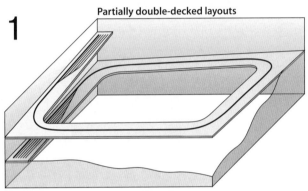

Point-to-point around the walls

Partially double-decked layouts

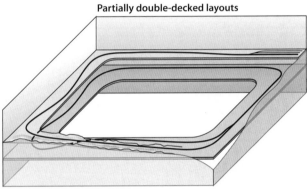

Continuous loop with branch line on upper level

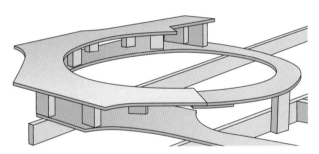

2 Helixes can be simple one-loop designs like this one, or they can be more complex, as fig. 3 shows.

Building a helix

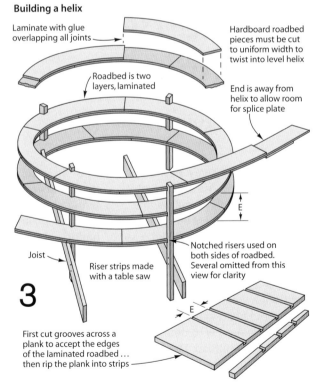

Laminate with glue overlapping all joints

Hardboard roadbed pieces must be cut to uniform width to twist into level helix

Roadbed is two layers, laminated

End is away from helix to allow room for splice plate

E

Joist

Riser strips made with a table saw

Notched risers used on both sides of roadbed. Several omitted from this view for clarity

E

3

First cut grooves across a plank to accept the edges of the laminated roadbed ... then rip the plank into strips

A BIG CONSIDERATION in adding a second deck is that the bracing for the upper deck must not interfere with scenery and operations on the lower level. (The lower level is the wall-mounted benchwork shown in Chapter 8.) There are a few ways of doing this, but we'll start by looking at common shelf brackets.

Figure 4 shows a cross-section drawing—you can adjust the dimensions to suit your installation. The distance between the top of the lower bracket and the bottom of the upper bracket is 16″. You can change this based on the height of your room, your height, and the type of scenery that you're planning.

You may be able to add shelf brackets directly to an existing wall; if not, use wall-mounted studs or 2 x 2s, as shown in Chapter 8. Standard stamped-metal utility brackets are inexpensive, unobtru-sive, and quite strong. Figure 5 shows how to mount them.

If you use a large bracket (the ones I used are 10″ x 12″), you might have to add a small length of 1 x 2 to the 2 x 2 to provide a solid surface area. It's important that screws in both upper mounting holes be anchored firmly. Make sure that the brace is level (fig. 6) before adding the second and third mounting screws.

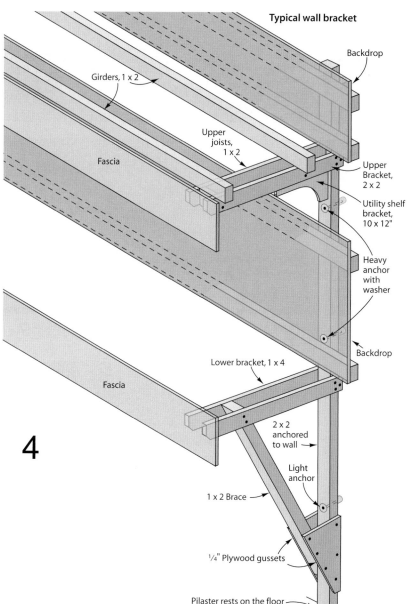

Typical wall bracket

Girders, 1 x 2

Upper joists, 1 x 2

Fascia

Backdrop

Upper Bracket, 2 x 2

Utility shelf bracket, 10 x 12"

Heavy anchor with washer

Backdrop

Lower bracket, 1 x 4

Fascia

2 x 2 anchored to wall

Light anchor

1 x 2 Brace

¼" Plywood gussets

Pilaster rests on the floor

4

5 Depending upon the width of the bracket, you may have to add a length of 1 x 2 to provide a wide enough mounting base.

6 Make sure the bracket is level, then screw it into place.

Add the horizontal 2 x 2 bracket arm as fig. 7 shows. This 2 x 2 is 16″ long; with a 12″ bracket you can safely extend this to about 18″ to 20″. If you need a deeper shelf, use a longer bracket. Screw this in place with three 1½″ drywall or round-head wood screws.

Add girders as fig. 8 shows. To save weight (and ¾″ of depth), use simple 1 x 2s on edge instead of L-girders. Use small lengths of vertical 1 x 1s to hold the girders to the bracket arms.

Add 1 x 2 joists and risers as with conventional L-girder bench-work (fig. 9), but use small 1 x 1 cleats on the sides of the girders to secure the joists.

Figure 10 shows the completed upper benchwork, with backdrop brackets added.

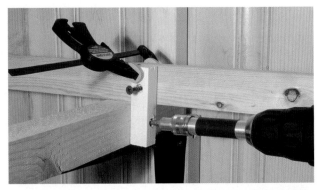

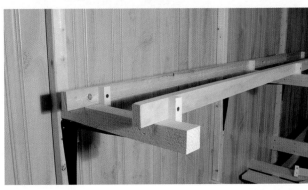

7 Drive screws through the stamped-metal brace into the 2 x 2.

8 Short lengths of 1 x 1s secure the vertical 1 x 2s to the bracket arms.

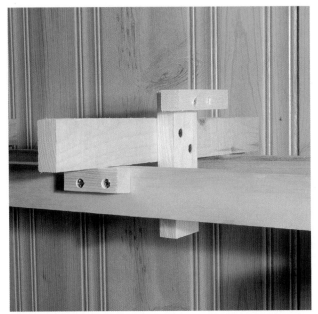

9 Joists and risers are added in the usual way, with small 1 x 1 cleats to hold the joists.

10 The upper shelf is complete, including horizontal 1 x 2s for mounting a backdrop.

THERE ARE SEVERAL other ways to mount the upper deck. If your upper deck is a flatland scene, you can simply lay ⅜″ or ½″ plywood over the 1 x 2 girders, as fig. 11 shows. Doing this saves a couple inches of depth.

Instead of shelf brackets you can use preformed and predrilled metal angle bars, as fig. 12 shows. These are quite strong and easy to use. The photo shows a single bar; I recommend using use one on each side of

the 2 x 2 for additional strength.

For the along-the-walls upper deck section of his HO Ohio Southern, Jim Hediger used a series of boxes (1 x 4 frames topped with ½″ plywood). As fig. 13 shows, these are mounted on simple brackets bolted to the walls, with brackets on arms at the joints.

For narrow (10″ or shallower) upper levels you can simply lay plywood directly on the shelf brackets themselves. Figure 14 shows a 7″-

wide shelf using 5″ x 6″ stamped-metal utility brackets.

Adding a front 1 x 2 lip shows adds strength and allows hiding wiring and splice plates behind the lip, resulting in a very clean look. With this design brackets are needed only every 32″ or so.

Bill Darnaby built his entire multi-deck layout using brackets, with extruded foam as the layout base. The sidebar on page 78 shows how he did it.

11 Flat plywood is a depth-saving alternative to joists and risers.

12 Preformed metal L-bars also work well for supporting brackets. Use one angle on each side of the bracket.

13 Jim Hediger uses frame boxes that slide into place on wall brackets and bracket arms.

14 Plywood can be mounted directly on shelf brackets for narrow shelves.

Foam on brackets

Bill Darnaby has built his multi-deck HO scale Maumee Route using the method shown in these photos and drawing. The brackets are Ls made from 1 x 2s and the layout base is 2"-thick extruded foam. The result is a very lightweight layout.

The brackets are spaced 16" apart. The shelf width can vary— Bill reports that bracket arms as long as 16" work well with 4" metal corner braces, but he has used arms as long as 24" with longer metal braces.

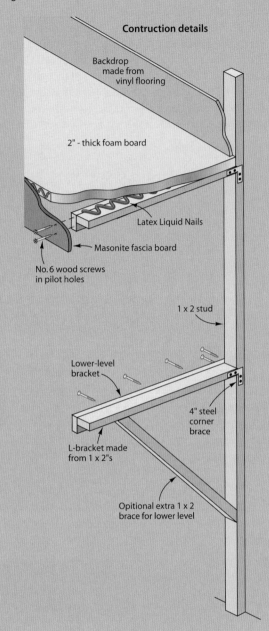

Contruction details

Backdrop made from vinyl flooring

2" - thick foam board

Latex Liquid Nails

Masonite fascia board

No. 6 wood screws in pilot holes

1 x 2 stud

Lower-level bracket

4" steel corner brace

L-bracket made from 1 x 2"s

Opitional extra 1 x 2 brace for lower level

BUILDING A DOUBLE-DECKED peninsula or free-standing layout presents some unique challenges. One method is to build an open-grid or L-girder table with a series of vertical 2 x 2s or 2 x 4s down the middle (fig. 15). The bracket arm can be a 1 x 3 or 1 x 4, depending upon the length of the bracket.

If the top level is open, with no backdrop, the 2 x 2 can be cut off at the top of the top bracket; if you need a backdrop, continue the 2 x 2 upward and mount horizontal 1 x 2s as backdrop brackets.

Jim Hediger built a double-decked peninsula on his HO Ohio Southern using an X-frame design as shown in fig. 16.

Jim notches a pair of 2 x 4s to make the X-frame itself. The inside top of the frame is then notched for the upper L-girders. The upper deck can extend quite far on either side of the girders, especially if 1 x 4 joists are used.

The result is an extremely strong layout that doesn't waste much space between the sides. Jim later adds a backdrop to hide the frame on the lower level.

Read on in Chapter 10 to see how backdrops and fascia can be used on multi-deck layouts.

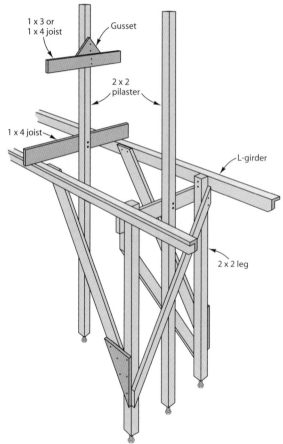

Free standing double-deck

1 x 3 or 1 x 4 joist

Gusset

2 x 2 pilaster

1 x 4 joist

L-girder

2 x 2 leg

15

16 Jim Hediger makes an X-frame using a pair of 2 x 4s for his free-standing double-deck benchwork.

10

Backdrops and fascia

Visually extend your layout

A backdrop is one of the most important scenic elements you can add to a layout. It takes up little room along the basement or room walls, but can visually extend a layout for miles.

Backdrops are extremely easy to add to an around-the-walls layout, and with proper planning they can be used on free-standing layouts as well. The key is to add the backdrop when you build the layout. Adding a backdrop after scenery is in place is difficult to do without damage.

Fascias are also important. They help define the lower edge of a scene, make layouts look clean by hiding supporting benchwork, and provide a place to hang throttles and mount switches and controls.

This chapter will take you through a couple ways of building both. Painting is beyond this book, but when you reach that step, I highly recommend Mike Danneman's book *Scenery for Your Model Railroad* (published by Kalmbach).

THE MOST COMMON material modelers use for backdrops is tempered hardboard (Masonite is one brand). It's an excellent choice— the ⅛"-thick material is smooth, resistant to warping or flexing once mounted, easy to handle, and easy to curve around corners. The sidebar on page 82 discusses other materials that can be used.

Start by making a frame for the backdrop. Having horizontal 1 x 2 supports at the top and bottom of the backdrop area will make the material easy to hang, as fig. 1 shows. Chapters 6 and 8 showed how to add these supports to vertical 1 x 2s or 2 x 2s.

1 Horizontal 1 x 2s at the top and bottom do an excellent job of supporting the backdrop.

2 Use a small piece of scrap wood to connect the brackets in the corner. Use two nails on one side of the bracket to keep the piece from twisting.

3 Each joint backing plate is a 1 x 4 with short 1 x 4s attached so they overhang each end.

4 Use a pair of screws top and bottom to secure the backing plate to the 1 x 2s

5 Clamp the first section of hardboard in place. Make sure the piece is horizontal.

6 Use a large twist bit and gentle pressure to make a dimple slightly larger than a screwhead.

Backdrop and fascia materials

• **Hardboard.** Tempered hardboard, ⅛" thick, is the most popular material for backdrops and fascia.

• **Sheet styrene.** Sheet styrene, .060" thick, works very well for backdrops. You can buy it in 4 x 8-foot sheets from plastics dealers in medium-size and larger cities. It installs like hardboard. Glue joints with plastic solvent and fill any gaps with plastic putty.

• **Drywall.** Drywall comes in 4-foot-wide sheets in 8-, 10-, 12-, and 14-foot lengths. A problem is that if you turn the sheet on its side you lose the beveled edges that make it so easy to join.

Drywall's biggest limitation is corners—it's very difficult to bend, so you'll need to use a different material to form corners.

• **Plywood.** Thin plywood can be used for a backdrop, but the wood grain tends to show through paint, even if using high quality (A) material. Also, even thin plywood is difficult to bend into corners.

• **Vinyl flooring.** This material comes in wide rolls, but cutoffs can often be had quite inexpensively from flooring stores. The color, pattern, and design don't matter—you mount it with the smooth underside facing outward. It easy to cut, but joints can be difficult.

The backdrop can extend an inch or two above the top without fear of sagging, and the bottom support can be five or six inches above the bottom of the backdrop.

For the best appearance make the backdrop as tall as possible. It should extend from the layout to the ceiling, if possible. Any open area between the top of the backdrop and the ceiling will be distracting, and it's no more difficult to install a 36"-tall backdrop than a 24" one. If your backdrop is 36" or taller, add a third 1 x 2 horizontal support down the middle.

Make sure the backdrop supports are connected at the corners as fig. 2 shows. A scrap of 1 x 2 or plywood works well to anchor them together. This will keep the backdrop from twisting or buckling at the corners.

Figure 3 shows how to prepare a backdrop joint. Make a backing plate from a piece of 1 x 4 cut to fit just between the top and bottom 1 x 2s. Add short pieces of 1 x 4 at the rear of each end of the backing plate so it can be screwed into place with the backing plate in the same plane as the 1 x 2 supports. Figure 4 shows the backing plate screwed into place. Don't install the backing plate until you're sure of the joint location.

Cut the hardboard to the proper width using a table saw or hand circular saw. Make sure that the ends are clean—if not, make a new cut to square them.

Avoid starting in a corner if possible. Avoid joints at corners—instead make sure the backdrop is flat for at least a foot on each side of a corner.

Place the first section in place and secure it with clamps. See fig. 5. It helps to have an assistant to get the pieces into place.

Attach the hardboard to the 1 x 2s with ¾" coarse-thread drywall screws. Use a ⅛" drill bit to make a pilot dimple in the face of the hardboard, as fig. 6 shows. It takes practice to do this correctly, so practice on some scraps first. Use very slow speed and light pressure, and pause frequently to check your progress.

Make sure you don't drill through the hardboard.

Drive the screws into place, as in fig. 7. Once again, go slowly, making sure that the screwhead is below the surface of the hardboard. Two reasons for using coarse drywall screws are that the head has a flatter profile than a wood screw, and the coarse threads bite well into the 1 x 2 with no pilot hole needed.

Add screws about every 8" along the top, but don't yet add the corner screw at the joint. Release the clamps at the splice plate, spread a coat of carpenter's glue under the hardboard, and reapply the clamps. Gluing the backdrop to the backing board makes it easier to get a clean joint and minimizes the chance of a joint cracking later.

Add screws down the splice plate, then remove the clamps again. Use a damp cloth or paper towel to remove any glue that oozed out. Add screws along the bottom strip to hold the hardboard in position.

Special backdrop situations

Free-standing backdrops can be done in much the same way as wall-mounted backdrops. See the drawing below. The important thing is to provide sufficient support—a series of vertical 2 x 2s is usually more than enough.

You can also use the backdrop to hide hidden tracks. The photo below shows one way to do it. The key to do this technique—called "wraparound staging"—is that the backdrop must be low enough that you can reach over and fix any problems that occur.

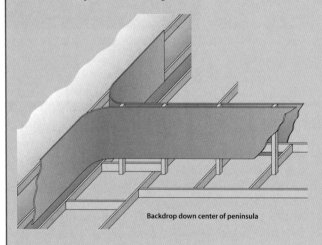

Backdrop down center of peninsula

The backdrop can be used as a viewblock to hide hidden track.

PLACE THE NEXT piece of hardboard in place, butting it tightly against the first. If the piece is to go around a corner, as the one in fig. 7, clamp it on that end, then keep pushing it to take the corner, clamping as you go. You can make the corner as broad as you wish, and with ⅛″ hardboard you can push the corner to about a 12″ radius.

Coming out of the corner, make sure that the backdrop is level, and continue clamping it until the end of the piece. You'll need another splice plate at the end.

Once the backdrop is in alignment, release the clamps at the end where it meets the first piece. Pull up the hardboard, spread glue on the splice plate, and replace the hardboard. Screw the backdrop into place as with the first piece. Be sure to add glue under the splice plate at the joint.

Continue adding additional backdrop sections around the layout in the same manner.

Once the backdrop is in place, begin cleaning and filling the screw holes and joints. Use a hobby knife to trim any loose fibers from the hardboard around the screw holes and joints (fig. 8).

Spackling compound works well to fill the screw holes and cracks. Apply it with a putty knife, as fig. 9 shows. Don't try to do the task with one coat. Instead, apply a coat, let it dry, sand any high spots, and add another coat. Repeat until the area is smooth.

Do joints in the same manner. A drywall sponge sanding block works well for sanding the spackle at the joint, as fig. 10 shows. Be sure to apply a coat of primer before painting your finish sky color on the backdrop. If any marks show through the primer, sand and reapply spackle until the area is smooth.

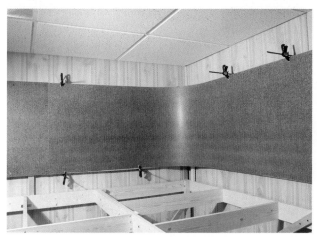

7 Clamp the second sheet in place so it butts tightly against the previous piece.

8 Use a knife to remove any fuzzy edges at joints and screw holes.

9 Use a putty knife to apply spackling compound above screwheads and at joints.

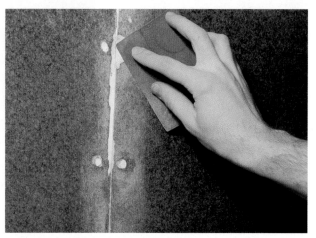

10 Smooth the spackling compound with sandpaper or a drywall sanding sponge. A second coat might be necessary.

A FASCIA, OR front board, added to a layout greatly cleans up the look of a layout. It looks much neater than bare wood or the edge of scenery. The fascia is also a great location for electrical switches, throttle jacks, throttle holders, holders for car routing cards, and small control panels.

Once again, hardboard is probably the most popular choice, and for good reason: it's relatively inexpensive, strong, easy to cut, smooth, and easy to paint.

Having the top of the fascia follow the scenery contour provides a clean, neat look. To do this you can either add the fascia before building any scenery, and then build the scenery can be to the fascia contours; or you can add the fascia after the scenery is in place. The methods remain the same.

The first step is to provide a solid mounting area for the fascia. This can be done in different ways, depending upon the benchwork method used. Figure 11 shows how

1 x 2 supports were added to the L-girder table from Chapter 3.

This isn't necessary—you could simply screw the fascia into the ends of the joists—but it will add some strength.

Open-grid layouts provide a firm base for the fascia, but depending upon the depth desired, you can add an additional 1 x 2 to give the fascia a bottom support point. See fig. 12.

Fascia depth is largely a matter of taste. Make it deep enough to hide

11 Several 1 x 2s have been added to this L-girder layout to provide a solid frame for a fascia.

12 On open-grid layouts, add an additional horizontal 1 x 2 to support the bottom of the fascia.

13 Clamp the hardboard fascia in place.

14 Use a marker to trace the scenery contour on the back of the hardboard.

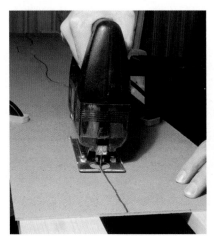

15 Use a saber saw to cut the fascia along the marked line.

16 Once the fascia is cut, clamp it in place against the side of the layout.

all of the upper benchwork components such as joists, and deep enough to hold all the controls and features you want. Making it too deep will restrict access under the layout.

Clamp the fascia material in place as fig. 13 shows. Trace the scenery contour onto the back of the fascia, as in fig. 14. If the scenery is in place, this is very easy. If the scenery isn't in place, it's best to guess a little on the high side so you can cut it lower if

necessary when you add scenery.

A saber saw works best for cutting the hardboard. See fig. 15. Cutting it with the back side toward the saw makes for a clean cut on the face, since the saber saw cuts on the upstroke.

Clamp the contoured fascia in place. See fig. 16. Once it's in position, you can install it in two ways. You can use countersunk screws (as described in the section on backdrops), filling the screw depressions with spackling compound.

A simpler method is to use wood screws with finishing washers, as fig. 17 shows. These provide a neat look, and are a good alternative, since the fascia doesn't require a perfectly smooth surface as on a backdrop.

Figure 18 shows both the fascia and backdrops installed on the double-deck layout shown in Chapter 9, and fig. 19 shows a contoured fascia on a finished layout.

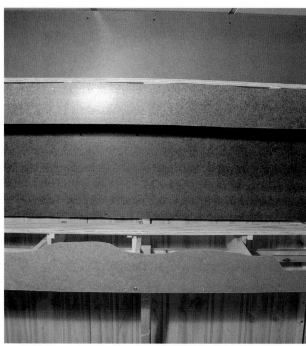

17 Wood screws with finishing washers are a good choice if you don't require a perfectly smooth finish.

18 Here's the double-deck benchwork from Chapter 9 with backdrops and fascia installed on both levels.

19 The deep fascia on Rick Rideout's HO Louisville & Nashville layout follows the lines of the scenery.

HAVING A FASCIA allows free-flowing curves around corners and peninsulas. See fig. 20. You can simply screw it to the ends of joists, and it will naturally follow the layout's contour. Another good example of this is on Monroe Stewart's N scale layout (fig. 21)

There are many ways to mount controls and other features on fascia. Figure 22 shows how Bill and Wayne Reid recessed a small control into the fascia on their N scale Cumberland Valley layout.

If you have hidden track on a lower level behind the fascia, you need to provide access in case of derailments. Sliding doors are good for long areas, and for smaller areas a small door with a magnetic catch works well, as fig. 23 shows.

20 Fascia can easily be made to follow the contour of the layout, as on Mike Danneman's N scale Rio Grande.

21 The curved fascia gives a smooth look to the peninsulas on Monroe Stewart's N scale layout.

22 The fascia on Bill and Wayne Reid's N scale Cumberland Valley includes recessed control panels and throttle jacks and hangers.

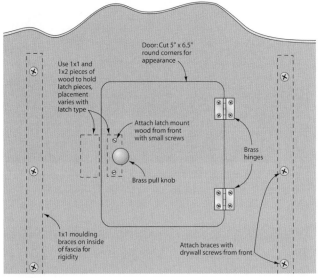

Door: Cut 5" x 6.5" round corners for appearance

Use 1x1 and 1x2 pieces of wood to hold latch pieces, placement varies with latch type

Attach latch mount wood from front with small screws

Brass hinges

Brass pull knob

1x1 moulding braces on inside of fascia for rigidity

Attach braces with drywall screws from front

23 A small door, with hinges mounted on the surface and a magnetic catch, works well to provide access to hidden track.

24 The area below the fascia can be left open or covered with a curtain, as on Don Gabrol's layout.

Duckunders, liftouts, and swinging gates

Options for gaining access to your layout

Most track-planning guides recommend avoiding duckunders, liftouts, and swinging gates if possible. However, we've all discovered at one time or another that to get optimum use from some spaces we have to locate the track across a door opening or other walkway.

To duck or not to duck

Should you leave an area as a duckunder? That depends upon how much ducking you'll have to do. If the bottom of the frame is fairly high (50″ or taller), and you and your operators are under 6 feet, ducking might not be too cumbersome.

There are couple of big advantages. First, it allows the bench-work to be continuous, with no worries about track alignment, as with gates or liftouts. Second, it allows seamless scenery and backdrops, with no breaks at the opening or duckunder area.

However, remember that the older we get the less agile we become. And, especially when dealing with an entrance to the layout, the annoyance of a duckunder could eventually diminish your overall enjoyment of the hobby.

Figure 1 shows a typical duckunder location. If you do choose a duckunder, here are some tips to keep in mind:

• Keep the layout at the duckunder area as narrow as you can (no more than 12″ if possible). The wider the duckunder is, the more likely it is that someone will rise too soon and bump it.

• Make the duckunder as tall as

11

possible. This sounds logical, but if you can use a 1 x 2 at that spot instead of 1 x 4 you'll save almost 2″ of height.

• Pad the underside of the duckunder, especially the edges. You can do this with rigid foam insulation, foam rubber covered with cloth, or other soft material. Be more concerned with safety than aesthetics.

• Brace the layout especially well at both ends of the duckunder area. Eventually you—or one of your crew—WILL hit your head or back on it, possibly with great force. Make sure everything is anchored to prevent damage or shifting of the layout.

• Label the area well to make sure people know that that is where they're supposed to enter and leave the layout.

One way to make a duckunder less cumbersome is by using the rolling chair technique. Leave a chair with rollers on it (such as an old office chair) at the duckunder location. As operators come and go they sit down in the chair and roll themselves under the duckunder, with minimal or no ducking required.

Liftouts

Probably the easiest way to design part of the layout as movable is to use a liftout section. Here are a few critical things to consider when building liftouts:

• Keep the span as short as possible.

• Keep the design as simple as possible. The more complex it is, the more likely something will get knocked out of alignment.

• Avoid turnouts on the liftout. If you absolutely must include them, make them manually operated.

• Have straight track at both ends (a curve in the middle is OK). Ninety-degree joints are best, but angles can still work well.

• Use care in lifting and replacing the section. Regardless of how sturdy the liftout is, the track can easily be dinged and knocked out of alignment.

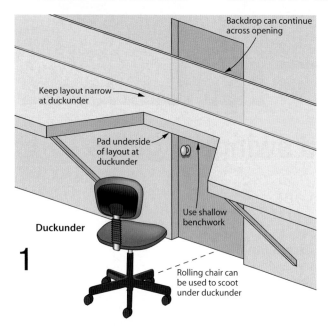

1 Keep layout narrow at duckunder
Backdrop can continue across opening
Pad underside of layout at duckunder
Use shallow benchwork
Duckunder
Rolling chair can be used to scoot under duckunder

2 This gap at a doorway requires a liftout section.

3 Cut the plywood so there's an even gap at each end.

4 Two short 1 x 2s laid flat across each end and a lengthwise 1 x 2 down the middle make up the bracing.

5 Screw a steel shelf mounting peg into each corner of the liftout section.

6 Clamp the 1 x 2 supports in place at each open end of the benchwork.

• Always, always, always check the track alignment every time you lock the liftout in place.

There are many ways of building liftout sections. This is one method that's worked for me, but feel free to come up with your own designs and modifications. Figure 2 shows the area requiring a liftout—crossing a doorway at the entry of the layout room.

Start by making sure that both ends where the liftout will connect are firmly anchored. Use a level to make sure that both ends are in alignment. On a free-standing layout, secure legs to the floor on each side.

The base for the liftout is a piece

of plywood. I used ⅜″; ¾″ is more solid but also heavy, and ½″ will work, but there's a better chance that it might have a slight warp or twist. The liftout doesn't necessarily have to be the same thickness as the subroadbed (in fact, it doesn't even have to be the same material). Choose as flat a piece of plywood as you can find.

Don't use dimensional lumber for the liftout. Dimensional lumber is too prone to warping and cupping as well as changing size along its length from changes in humidity.

Cut the piece to fit. Mine is 6″ wide by 32¼″ long; you'll have to adjust the dimensions to fit your application. The gap between each

end and the subroadbed on the layout should be about ³⁄₃₂″. See fig. 3.

Figure 4 shows the bracing under the plywood. A 1 x 2 across each end provides a stable base, and a lengthwise 1 x 2 down the middle of the bottom provides longitudinal strength and serves as a handle for grabbing the liftout. Glue each piece and screw them into place from the top.

Round the corners of the lengthwise 1 x 2 with a plane or Surform tool, then sand it to eliminate any chance of getting splinters while handling the piece.

Steel shelf pegs on angles work well as locating pins. I used ³⁄₁₆″-diameter pins, but you can change

7 Use a pencil to color the ends of the pins, then align the liftout and press on the ends to mark the support 1 x 2s.

8 Drill a hole at each of the pin marks. Use a drill press if possible.

9 A T-handle reamer makes it easy to enlarge the top of each hole.

10 Adjust the alignment of the 1 x 2 end supports with the liftout pressed firmly in place.

11 A hook and eye at each end hold the liftout securely in place.

this based on what you can find at your local hardware store. Mount a peg at each corner, as fig. 5 shows.

Clamp a support base (a length of 1 x 2) in place on each side of the opening (fig. 6). Round the ends of these pieces by cutting them at an angle, then shaping them with a Surform and sandpaper.

Mark the locations of the pin locator holes by first coloring the ends of the pins with a pencil, as in fig. 7. Place the liftout gently into place, making sure it is aligned properly, with an equal gap at each end.

Press the liftout firmly against the support 1 x 2s at each end, taking care not to alter the alignment. The result will be four visible pin marks.

It's important that these holes be drilled perpendicular to the resting surface, so use a drill press

if possible. See fig. 8. Using a ³⁄₁₆″ bit (or one to match your pins) drill the hole at least twice as deep as the pin.

Enlarge the hole slowly using a T-handle reamer, as fig. 9 shows. This makes the hole larger at the top, allowing the pins to slide in easily but still holding them firmly. Use a spare pin to check the hole as you're reaming it. It should slip in easily, but the last ⅛″ or so should be snug.

Press the support base 1 x 2s onto the pins and place the liftout in position. Use clamps to hold the supports in place while you adjust the height and alignment. See fig. 10. Use a straightedge to make sure that the top of the liftout is at exactly the same level as the roadbed. Once both ends are aligned, use three 1½″ no. 8 wood screws to hold each in place.

Once the liftout section is in place, you need to be sure that it stays firmly locked into alignment. To do this I used a very low-tech but effective device, a 2½″ hook and eye. See fig. 11.

Screw the hook to the benchwork and locate the eye on the long 1 x 2 on the liftout. You want it loose enough that it's not difficult to hook, but tight enough that it exerts a pull to keep the liftout firmly in position.

Use the same type of roadbed across the liftout as on the layout, and make sure the height matches. I prefer to use sectional track (instead of flex) at the joint, as the rigidity of sectional track helps keep things in solid alignment.

Use track nails to secure the track, with a gap of ¹⁄₁₆″ between the rail ends on the liftout and layout. See fig. 12.

12 Lay the track on the liftout and on each end of the layout. Use sectional track and leave a ¹⁄₁₆″ gap between rail ends.

13 Mount a push-button switch at the proper height so that the liftout will trigger it when in place. An old cabinet magnet case houses the push button.

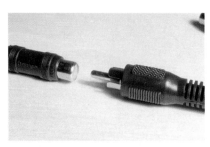

14 A two-connector plug and socket can be used to provide power to the liftout.

15 The angles on each end of the bridge enable a tight clearance between rail ends on the bridge and layout.

Electrical connections

You want to be certain that you or one of your operators doesn't accidentally run a train over the edge if the liftout isn't in place—a primary concern with a liftout.

The best way to limit this possibility is to add a switch that kills the power to surrounding track sections when the liftout is lifted out. Figure 13 shows one way of doing this using a miniature single-pole, single-throw, normally open push-button switch.

Route the track power to the adjoining block through the switch. When the liftout is in place, the switch is pushed in, completing the circuit. As soon as the section is lifted out, the switch pops up, breaking the circuit and stopping any locomotives near the opening.

You also need to supply electricity to the liftout itself. Figure 14 shows one way of doing it. A two-connector wire with a plug can be connected to a socket on the layout. Once the section is in place, plug the connector in place and you're ready to go.

You can also use contact plates between the liftout and the layout to route electricity, or use a couple of magnetic cabinet latches as described in the sidebar on this page.

Alternative liftout methods

There are other ways to secure liftout sections. Bill Darnaby uses cabinet magnet latches to align and secure a liftout on his HO Maumee Route. Bill has even used this method for a curved liftout section.

Swinging gates

Another way to cross a gap is to hinge a section of the layout, allowing it to swing open to allow passage. The big advantage of a swinging gate over a liftout is that a gate stays secured to the layout: You don't have to find a place to set it when it's not connected.

Probably the biggest disadvantage is potential alignment problems. Also, depending upon how it's installed, it can get in the way and be bumped while open.

The best gate design I've ever used is on Gary Hoover's HO layout. Figure 15 shows Gary's bridge.

The key to the design is the angles on both the hinge and free end of the gate, which allow the gate rails to move away from the fixed rails on the layout.

Magnetic liftout

When Bill Darnaby needed a curved liftout section for his HO Maumee Route, he decided to use magnetic cabinet latches to align the bridge, lock it in place, and conduct electricity. The technique would work well for a straight section as well.

The two photos tell the whole story. The liftout itself is a piece of ¾" plywood cut to fit (about 30" long). On each end two magnets serve as the base with a third on edge to lock the side in place (the matching steel plates are secured to the liftout). Bill had to adjust the magnets a bit to eliminate any play or wobble in them.

Track power is fed through the magnets and picked up on the liftout by the steel plates.

Bill laid the track across the bridge, then used a motor tool with a cutoff wheel to cut gaps in the rails at each end.

Benchwork as furniture

Making your layout room an attractive setting

We often view benchwork as utilitarian, and although we occasionally perk it up with shelves or painted fascia, few of us pay much attention to the room beyond the layout itself.

There's another direction we can go, making the benchwork—and the layout itself—an attractive centerpiece to a rec room or other living area. This can be as simple as placing a layout atop homemade or commercial bookshelves, or as complex as integrating it with a museum-quality display.

Making your layout room or area as attractive and welcoming as pos-

sible will draw you to the space, perhaps inspiring you to spend more time and do more work on your layout.

Improving the room by finishing walls, adding carpeting or other flooring, adding a finished ceiling, installing good lighting, or decorating with railroad-theme artwork all can be good steps to take.

Here are a few examples of modelers who have taken extra steps to make their benchwork more than just lumber that holds up a layout. I hope you're able to get some ideas from them that you can use on your own railroads

Dick Patton has a very impressive On3 layout, but what makes his layout so striking is the way the layout is presented. The benchwork—and indeed, the whole basement structure—is designed as a small museum, with the layout just a small but integral part of the whole picture.

Dick collects all sorts of railroad memorabilia, including headlights, station signs, lanterns, number boards, station furniture, and many other items. Designing the whole basement around this theme makes it a very attractive area.

As the photo shows, he has integrated a dispatcher's/agent's office into the scene, and carried the typical old-fashioned wainscoting and woodwork around the basement and along the benchwork. This helps tie everything together.

All of the memorabilia and other items are attractively displayed, and although there's a lot of stuff there, it looks very neat.

Most important, Dick's basement is a place that's inviting—it looks like it would be very enjoyable to spend time there, regardless of whether or not model trains are running.

When Mike Tylick built his O scale Pioneer Valley layout (a *Model Railroader* project layout), he designed the benchwork to do much more than support trains. He built it atop cabinets designed to hold trains, books, and other items, and by doing so made it a very attractive piece of furniture.

Mike's layout is 12 feet long, comprising two 6-foot-long, 18"-wide sections. He built his own cabinets using dimensional lumber and plywood as the photo shows, then painted it. Mixing cabinet styles—wide shelves, narrow shelves, and enclosed sections with doors—gives the benchwork a varied look and makes it appear longer than it is.

Although Mike built his own cabinets, it would certainly be possible to do the same by using commercial modular shelves and cabinets as sold at various home building centers.

Above: Mike Danneman shows us another way to showcase a layout and memorabilia in his basement. The N scale layout dominates the scene, and although the fascia isn't yet painted, the broad curves of the fascia give the layout a smooth, clean look.

Mike has displayed his memorabilia neatly both above and below the layout. By doing this, and keeping the layout area clean, neat, and bright, he has created a space that looks like a pleasant place to spend time.

Left: This photo illustrates another attractive use of a small shelf. Bill and Mary Miller located a staging yard for their On3 layout in their family room, which is adjacent to the layout room. The railroad is an attractive addition to the room, which also serves as a crew lounge/waiting area on operating nights.

Bottom: Another good example of a very neat railroad setting in a small space is Swedish modeler Lars-Göran Larsson's HO layout on a bookshelf. A layout such as this would be attractive and yet quite unobtrusive in a living room, rec room, or bedroom.

The layout and scenery are all built along one shelf of a long, shallow bookshelf fixture. Small fluorescent fixtures provide the lighting.

The same concept could be used in a number of styles of commercial or home-made bookshelves of any length.